Easy "No-Bake"

HOLIDAY WISH HOUSE

and
Other
Holiday Houses

*Written and Illustrated
by Teresa Morgan*

Dorrance Publishing Co., Inc.
Pittsburgh, Pennsylvania 15222

$\mathcal{M}$y mother Mary, you are in my heart and in my mind every day, and my family, Niles, Heather and Sarah, who without their love, understanding, patience and fondness of take out food, this book would not exist.

♥

Patty,
May all your
Holiday Wishes come
true
Terri Morgan · 96

TABLE OF CONTENTS

Dear Friends,

This is the book that you have been looking for. It is a very simple guide to teach you how to make an "Easy NO-BAKE Holiday Wish House."

When my oldest daughter was in third grade, she came home from school one day and asked what kind of Christmas traditions our family had. Well, I thought and thought; and all that I could come up with was the old Christmas-cookie-and-decorate-the-tree routine. It didn't seem very exciting or traditional; so, being the wonderful mother that I am, I asked her, "Well, what Christmas tradition would you like to have, honey?" With those beautiful, big blue eyes, she looked up at me and said, "How about a gingerbread house?" "Oh," I said. Well, I was stuck again. I was never very good at things you had to roll out and bake, but again being the wonderful mother that I am, I said, "Sure." So out came the cookbooks with all of the wonderful recipes for gingerbread and all of the patterns for the houses that needed to be cut out ahead of time and all of the directions that were labeled "Day 1" and "Day 2." (They had to be kidding!)

Well, still being the wonderful mother that I am, I proceeded to make my first two gingerbread houses. During the process, my daughter—looking at me with her beautiful, big blue eyes—said, "Why don't we invite some of my friends and have a gingerbread house decorating party?" I said, "Sure." Now my two houses turned into six houses, and there I was until two o'clock in the morning with patterns and cardboard and rolling pins and flour and a very bad attitude. Finally I was finished with my six houses and went to bed exhausted. The next morning, I awoke to find that my houses had collapsed. There I was with no houses, a very sad, little blue-eyed daughter and five little girls that would be coming in a few days to decorate and start this wonderful Christmas tradition.

Okay, there had to be and easier way. Over to the pantry I went. Let's see, what is brown? Uh huh...graham crackers. I sat down with my box of crackers, my tube of icing, and away I went. Not only did we have a decorating party that year, but we have had it every year since, and it has gotten bigger and better each year!

I hope that by following these easy instructions, you too will be able to start a wonderful holiday tradition to help make all of your holiday wishes come true.

Happy Holidays,

Terri Morgan

CHAPTER 1

Just a
Few Hints

 # Just a Few Hints

1. Read all of the instructions first.
2. Assemble all of your supplies.
3. Cover your base before you begin if desired.
4. Don't do this on a rainy or humid day. The icing will not dry properly, and you will have problems later.
5. Sometimes if you use heavy candies on the roof, it will tend to sag in the center and at the tips. Do not disturb it during the drying time. Chances are it will dry in the sagging position. This had happened to me on a number of occasions, and it looks just fine.
6. Some candies will tend to bleed after they are placed on the house. There isn't very much you can do about this. Unfortunately you won't know which candies will do it until they are on the house.
7. Remember to choose candies that are no larger than a quarter, choosing no round gum ball-type candies. Round candies tend to look too large on the house and will want to roll down the side of the house.
8. Suckers are also something that I had trouble with. After one day, they would run. They do look cute, and you still could use them, but you would have to leave the wrappers on.
9. If you use candy canes along the roof edge, do not cover the house with plastic wrap to transport it. The plastic wrap tends to stick to some candy canes.
10. Keep the house out of sunlight. It will melt any chocolate that is on the house.
11. Coconut is not a good choice if you plan on saving your house for the next year. When you spray the house, the coconut becomes damp again; and when you take it out the next year, you take the chance of it being mildewed.
12. I also recommend not using nuts if you plan on keeping the house. They have natural oil that tends to seep through the spray.

13. Chocolate looks good and tastes great. However if you plan on freezing your house, remember that it will turn white in the freezer.

14. Wipe up any icing that you get on the work surface as soon as possible. It does dry very hard and will be harder to clean up later.

15. Keep a bowl of hot water in your sink in which to put your beaters, spoons, etc. This will melt the icing and make it easier to clean up.

16. Keep any icing that is left in the bowl covered with a damp cloth. It will crust over very quickly and begin to harden in about 10 minutes.

17. Don't be afraid to use lots of icing—the more, the better. Pretend that it is glue. After all, that is basically what it is.

18. Don't worry about being sloppy. You can cover mistakes with more icing or candy later.

19. If a piece of candy falls off after the icing has dried, use a new piece of candy.

20. Sometimes, because of the combined weight of the icing and candy on the ends of the roof, the tips will break off. If this happens, don't get upset. Remember that the icing is like glue. You can fix almost anything. Find a mug or glass that will fit right under the end tip of the roof. Put icing on the part that broke off; press it into place; and push the mug or glass up underneath the end tip. Let it dry for a long time. Carefully remove the mug. If it breaks off again, just follow the same procedure.

21. Remember to decorate in the following order: front, one side, back, the other side, one roof section, the other roof section and finally the yard. I have found over the years that I don't get in my own way if I decorate in this order.

22. Put a nice, big icing dot under the reinforcement pieces. This will give a little added strength.

23. Try not to eat too much of this icing; it is very sweet.

24. Try to place all of your windows and shutters at the same level around your house. It will make the appearance more pleasing to the eye.

25. Sandwich-type cookies tend to separate. Stay with wafers, tea, shortbread or any flat cookie.
26. Attach all candies, cookies, pretzels, etc. with icing.
27. Do not use extra large eggs in this recipe.
28. If the icing does not want to stiffen, add one-half cup more powdered sugar and one–half tsp. cream of tartar.

CHAPTER 2

Preparation

 # **Preparation**

To make a Christmas Wish House, you will need...

> 1 BOX OF GRAHAM CRACKERS
> 2 LBS. OF POWDERED SUGAR
> 6 EGG WHITES
> 1 TSP. CREAM OF TARTAR
> A BASE
> A LARGE MIXING BOWL
> ELECTRIC MIXER
> DISPOSABLE CAKE DECORATING BAGS
> ICING KNIFE
> MEASURING SPOONS
> STRAIGHT PIN
> TAPE
> SCISSORS
> EXTRA CONTAINER
> PAPER TOWELS
> LOTS OF YOUR FAVORITE CANDIES

SELECTING YOUR BASE

Your base should measure at least 13" or 14" square or round, whichever you prefer. Cardboard works quite nicely. If you have a pretty tray that you would like to be visible around your finished house, this also works very well. There is no need to worry about scratching the surface of your tray because any icing that is left on the tray after you have enjoyed sharing your house with your family and friends can simply be soaked off later. Cover or select your base and set it aside.

GRAHAM CRACKERS

I use any name brand graham cracker. Remember, though, that humidity does play a part in drying time; so try to work on a day when the humidity is low and it is not raining. Make sure that you read the label on the side of the box to be certain that the crackers come in blocks of four crackers and not in blocks of two, or you will be sticking crackers together forever.

DECORATING BAGS

I like to use plastic disposable decorator bags that you can find at your local cake decorators' store or the housewares department of your local department store. They are very inexpensive and very convenient. After you are finished, just throw them away. If you have a little cake decorating experience and want to get a little fancy with your house, you can also put couplers and tips in the ends of these bags. One recipe of icing fills three disposable bags, more than enough to decorate your Holiday Wish House.

CHAPTER 3

Magic Icing

 # Magic Icing

This is a very simple icing recipe that almost anyone can make and very seldom fails. Its only enemy is humidity.

You need....

6 Egg whites
2 Lbs. of powdered sugar
1 Tsp. cream of tartar

In a large mixing bowl, dump in the 6 egg whites. Right on top, dump in your 2 lbs. of powdered sugar and 1 tsp. cream of tartar.

Set your mixer at the very slow speed at first. If you turn it on too fast, it will snow in your kitchen.

At first the icing will look very gummy, but be patient. After the powdered sugar is completely mixed in, turn your mixer on high and continue to mix until it is very stiff.

When you stop your mixer, the icing should not move. It should have a very pretty satiny look to it. (Figure 3-1). It's hard to give a time as to how long to beat it. If you use a standard mixer, it whips up quicker than if you use a portable or hand mixer.

3-1

Fill your bags immediately. But DO NOT cut off the tips until you are ready to use them. If you have never filled an icing bag before, here is how to do it.

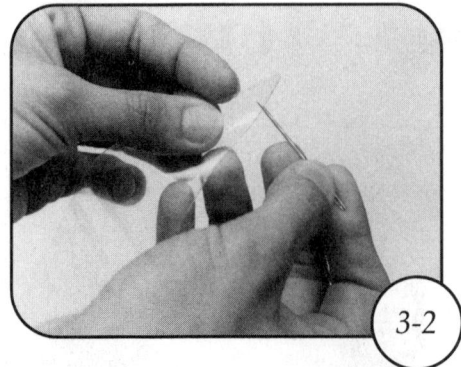

If your are using a disposable, plastic icing bag, put a small pin hole at the pointed end of the bag (Figure 3-2). This helps to release air that is trapped in the bag as you push your icing down.

3-2

Now fold or cuff the wide end of the bag down about two inches. Open the bag up to form a cone.

With a long icing knife, scoop the icing out of the mixing bowl and drag the knife along the inside of the open icing bag (Figure 3-3).

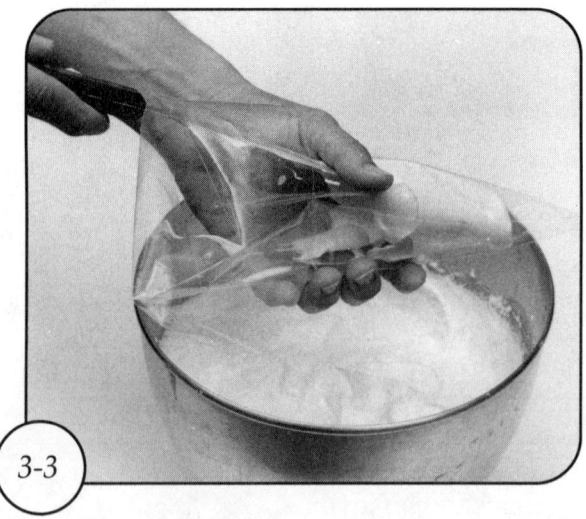

3-3

When the bag is two–thirds full, unfold the cuffed end and twist the end until the icing begins to move farther down into the bag.

Let any trapped air release itself through the pinhole (Figure 3-4).

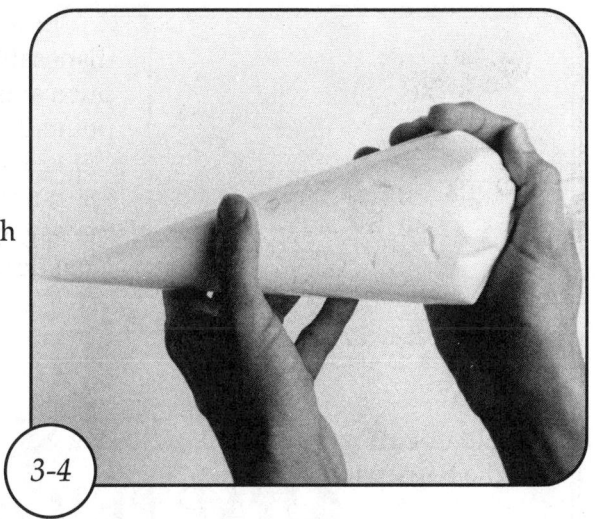

3-4

3-5

Now either tape or keep the wide end of the bags twisted shut (Figure 3-5).

This is very important because the icing will begin to crust over in a matter of about 10 minutes and begin to harden in about 20 minutes. If you do not wish to fill all of your bags at once, just cover the icing left in the bowl with a damp paper towel.

CHAPTER 4

Making the
House Sections

 # Making the House Sections

Now it is time to put the sections of the house together. The first time that you make this house, I suggest that you do it in three stages. The first is to assemble the sections and let them dry. The second is to assemble the house and let it dry. The third, and the most fun, is to decorate. I make this suggestion not because the house is difficult to assemble, but by allowing a little more drying time on your first house, your chances of any of the sections falling apart are a lot less. As you do more houses, you will be able to shorten the drying time.

Unwrap one whole box of graham crackers and check for cracks and breakage. Set any damaged ones aside in an extra container. (You will be able to use the damaged crackers later on.) Make sure, as you lay your crackers down on your counter or table, that all of your crackers are on the same side. You will notice that one side of the crackers is a little flatter than the other. Decide which side of the cracker you want to show on the "outside" of your house, and lay that side face down on your surface. This may not sound like a very important point, but it does make a difference in the appearance of your finished house. Also make sure that the reinforced seams of the house sections are in a horizontal position. This makes the appearance of the house more uniform.

WALLS AND ROOF

One box of crackers will normally make:

2 Roof sections   2 Side sections

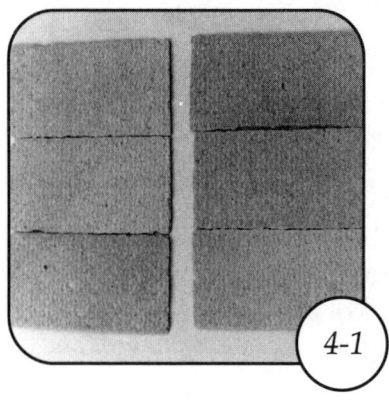

4-1

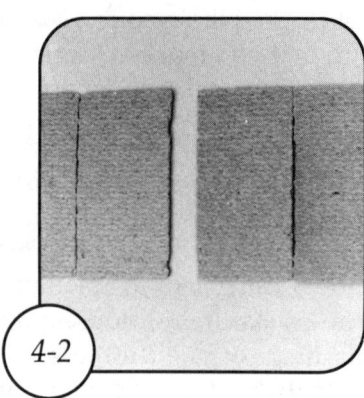

4-2

1 Front and
1 Back section

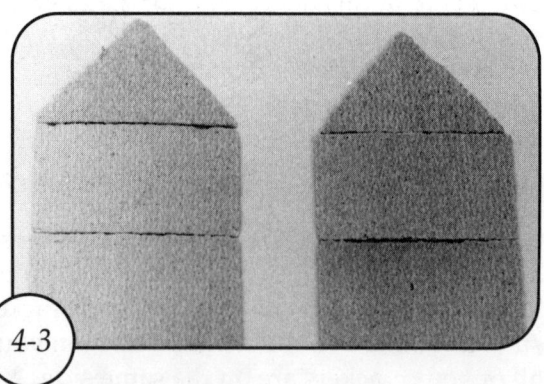

4-3

The diagrams below will be used throughout this book:

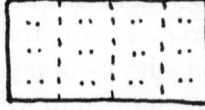   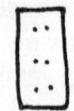

1 Cracker   1/2 Cracker   1/4 Cracker

MITERS

Line up the house sections on your work surface as shown in the preceding illustrations. Now you need to cut your mitered pieces for the roof sections. This may be the most difficult part of assembling the whole house, but be patient. Practice on a few pieces first. If you make any mistakes, just save the pieces; you may be able to use them later.

To make the front and back mitered pieces, you need a sharp serrated knife. If you look closely, the cracker has one flat side and one raised side. Place the flat side down on your work surface. Be careful not to press too firmly on the cracker's center line.

This is the weakest part of the cracker, and it is very easily broken at this point. Simply hold the cracker with your fingers separated on either side of this line. You do not need to cut all the way through the cracker. All that you need to do is very carefully score a diagonal line from the center of your cracker to the opposite edge (Figure 4-4).

Turn your cracker and score another diagonal line from the opposite outside corner to the center (Figure 4-5).

Now gently break the cracker on the diagonal cut that you just made doing one side first (Figure 4-6)

4-6

and then the other (Figure 4-7).

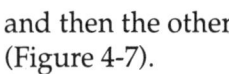

4-7

Save the small pieces; you can use them for a chimney later.

Your crackers should all be lined up on your work surface with the side that you want on the outside of your house face down.

Cut off about a 1/2" piece from the tip of one of your icing bags. Starting with your roof section, gently hold the first and second crackers together with one hand while you apply a nice big drop of icing right in the center of the seam (Figure 4-8).

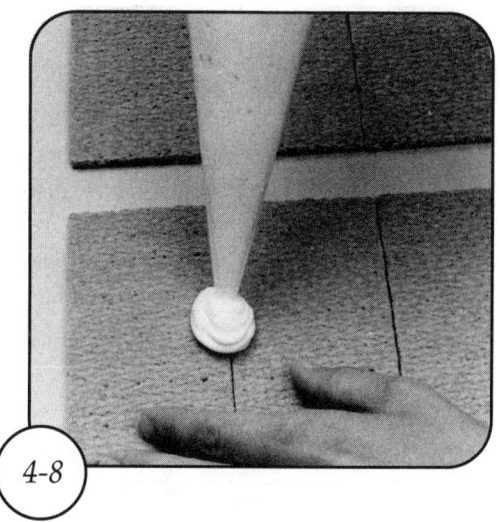

4-8

You want to hold them together as you apply the icing so that, as you are applying the icing, the pieces don't separate.

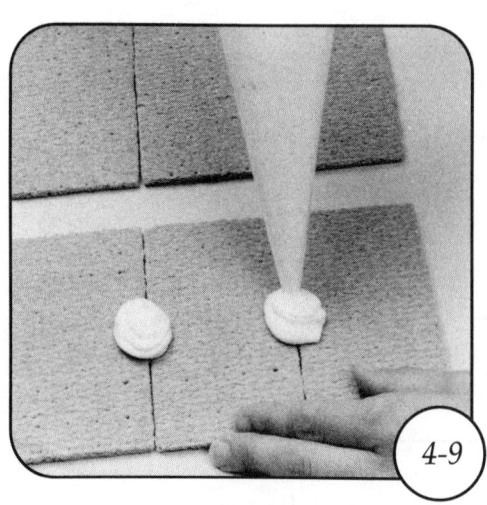

4-9

Continue to do this to the rest of the seams of both roof sections (Figure4-9).

Now break about a 1" (no larger) square piece of cracker from the damaged pieces that you saved earlier.

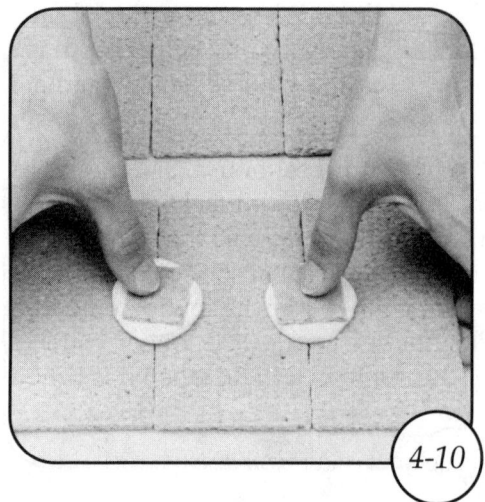

Place one on top of each drop of icing. Hold the ends of the crackers with your fingers as you gently press the 1″ piece down with your thumbs (Figure 4-10). Again, you want to hold the ends of the crackers with your fingers so that when you press down, your crackers do not separate.

4-10

Use this same procedure with the two side sections and the front and back sections. Here, however, you may use larger reinforcement pieces, approximately one-forth of a graham cracker.

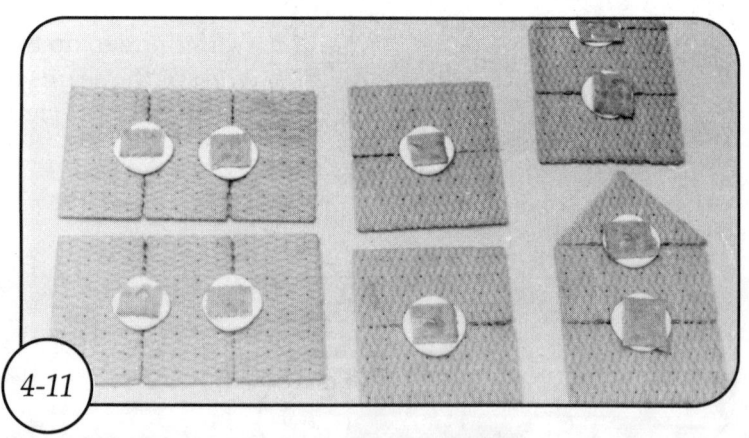

4-11

This is all the reinforcement that you need on the inside of this house (Figure 4-11).

Surprisingly, when it dries,it is very strong and completely edible. There is no need for any other kind of reinforcement at all.

Let this dry for about 5 minutes and then slide each section about an inch across your work surface. This breaks any icing that may have seeped through as you were pressing your sections together away from your work surface.

Now let these sections dry. If this is your first house, I suggest that you let them set at least two hours, longer if you feel more comfortable. You want them to be firm enough so that when you pick up your sections, they don't break apart at the seams. If this happens, simply add a little more icing under the reinforcement piece, press down again and let dry. Of course, the longer you let it dry, the harder and stronger the sections will be when it is time to assemble the house.

Go sit down, have a cup of coffee and relax; *you deserve it!*

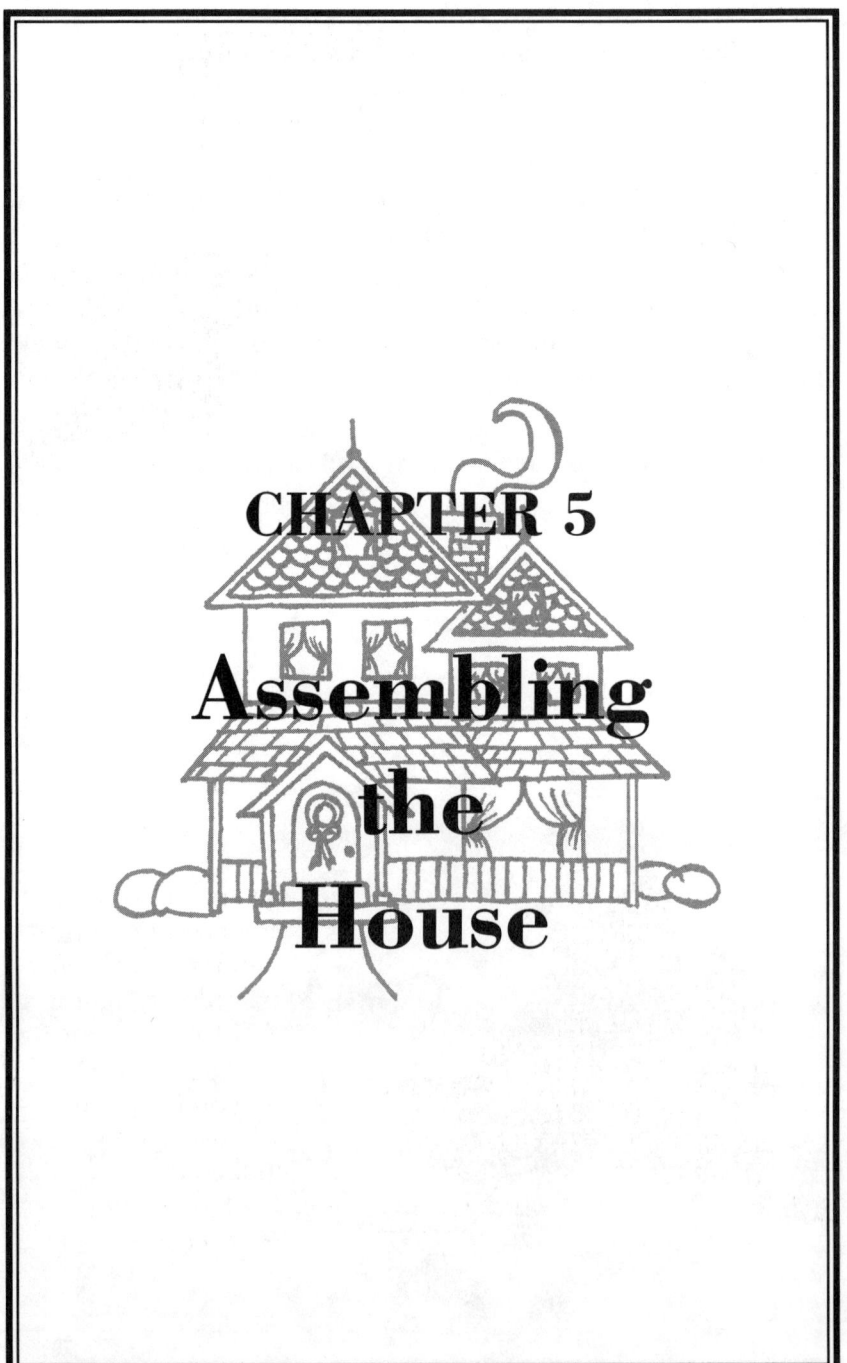

CHAPTER 5

Assembling the House

Assembling the House

WALLS

Choose one of your end sections as the front of your house and run a bead of icing from just under the top of the mitered piece to the bottom on both sides (Figure 5-1).

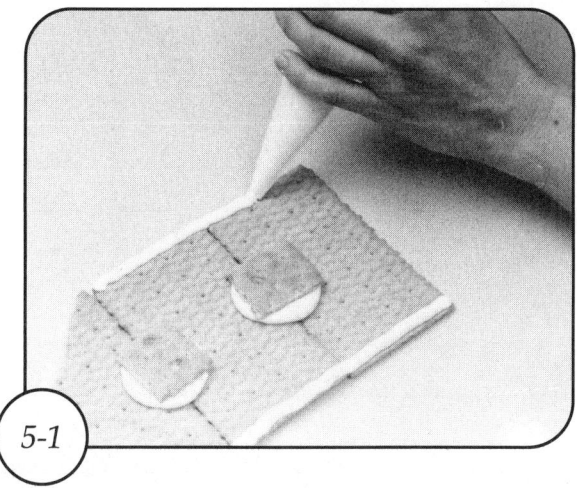

5-1

Now carefully pick this front piece up in your left hand. Don't be afraid of it; if it is nice and firm, it will not break apart.

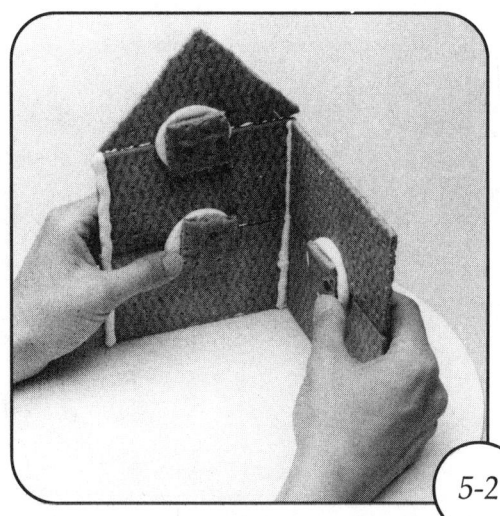

5-2

While you are holding the front section in your left hand, pick up a side section in your right hand. Place the front section on the base where you would like your house to be positioned (center, forward, back more to one side, etc.) (Figure 5-2).

I usually set it back a little so that I have more room in the front for trees, fences, shrubs, etc. Next, press the side section onto the bead of icing on the front section. If your icing is nice and stiff, it will catch very easily and stay inplace.

5-3

Then run a bead of icing all along the inside wall of the front and side sections (Figure 5-3).

This helps to anchor the house to the base.

Attach the other side of the house to the front section in the same manner. Run a bead of icing along the inside of this piece.

Picture an imaginary line that connects the back section to the side sections, and run a bead of icing along your base (Figure 5-4).
Run a bead of icing along both sides of the back section as you did the front section (Figure 5-1) and carefully put this last house section into place.

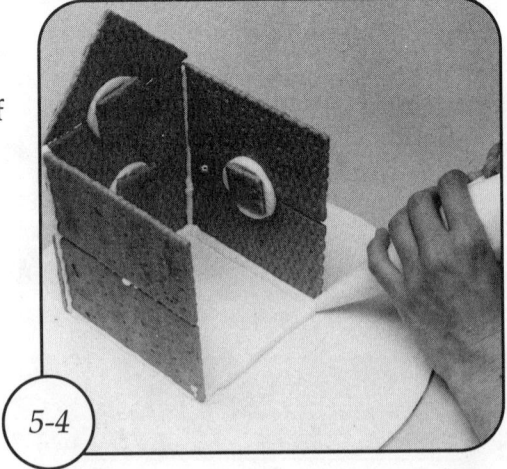

5-4

24

Stand over your house and, looking into it, square it up as best you can (Figure 5-5).

It does not need to be perfect because a lot, if not all, of your mistakes will be covered up with icing later on.

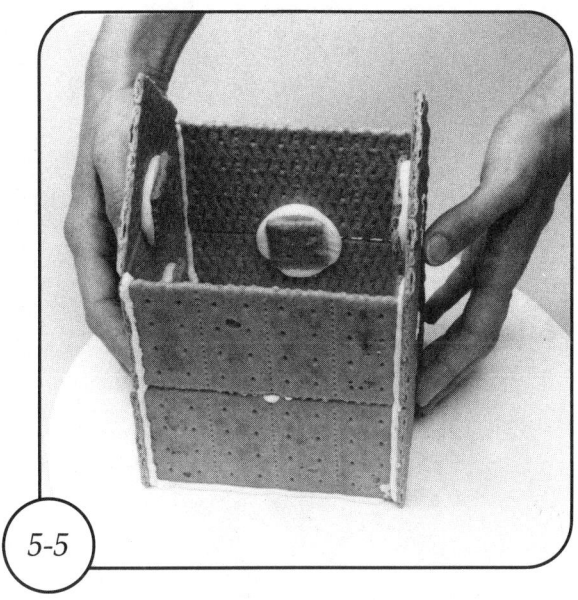

5-5

ROOF

Attaching the roof sections is very easy as long as the seams of the roof are hard and dry.

5-6

Run a bead of icing along both mitered edges of the front and back sections (Figure 5-6).

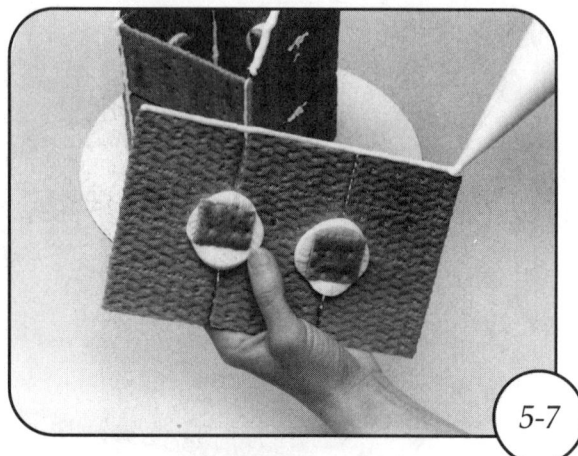

Carefully pick up a roof section and run a bead of icing along one of the long edges that you choose to be the top of the roof (Figure 5-7).

5-7

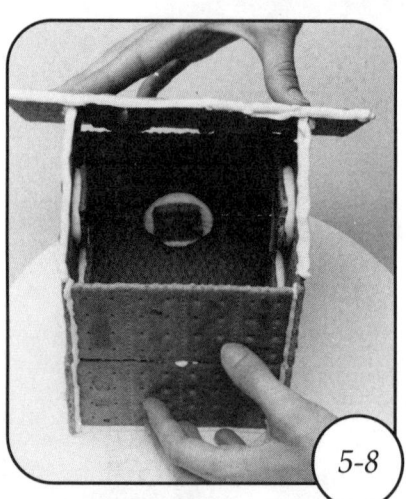

Place this roof section on the side of the house along the mitered edge, trying to center it along the front and back edge(Figure 5-8).

5-8

Attach the other roof section in the same manner.

After you have made sure that they are both centered, gently press them in place (Figure 5-9).

5-9

Bend over and check under the roof to make sure that you don't have any space between the roof sections and the front and back sections.

If you do, you may simply fill these in with more icing (Figure 5-10).

5-10

Finally run a last bead of icing all along the outside base of the house to make sure that it will be anchored securely to the base (Figures 5-11 and 5-12).

5-12

5-11

There you have it! Your very own Holiday Wish House is all finished and ready to be decorated. Give it a chance to dry a little before you begin to decorate. Aren't you proud of yourself? CONGRATULATIONS!

CHAPTER 6

Making a House

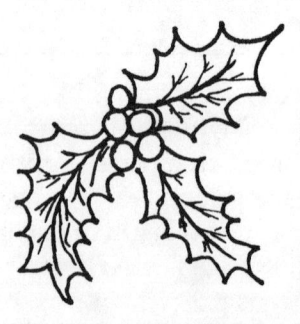

 # Making a House

YOU WILL NEED:

Green food coloring
Small candy canes
Large candy canes
Fruit sheet
Lifesavers
Peppermint candies
Chocolate bars
Small gumdrops
Wax paper
Red cinnamon candies
Round jelly rings
Bought pretzel men
Small ice cream cones
Large ice cream cones
Sprinkles
Red or green jelly beans

If you cannot find all of these supplies,
you may substitute with other candies.

LET'S BEGIN

Before you begin, please remember that this is a very simple house with basic decorations and simple ideas. Please feel free to change or elaborate with your own decorating as we go.

Find yourself a nice relaxing spot to work in. Some people like to stand when they work; some like to sit. The more comfortable you can make yourself, the more enjoyable this will be for you. Get yourself something to drink. No matter how hard you try not to eat the candy, some of it will disappear; and you will probably do a lot of finger licking too. Oh, well...the diet can start tomorrow.

Prepare the icing. Put it in bags, twist the ends shut tight and tape them closed. Set these aside.

Fill the mixing bowl used for icing with hot water and set it in your sink. Soak your beaters, icing knife and any other utensils that you use in the hot water. This makes cleanup easy later on. Set the finished house in front of you.

6-1

Set your candies next to your house. Open any bags and unwrap any candy now. This saves time later while you are decorating (Figure 6-1).

I like to make my trees, wreaths, shutters and windows first. This gives them time to set, and it is also easier to assemble them on the work surface rather than on the house.

TREES

Tint about 1 cup of icing green. Hold an ice cream cone upside down and frost thickly (Figure 6-2).

6-2

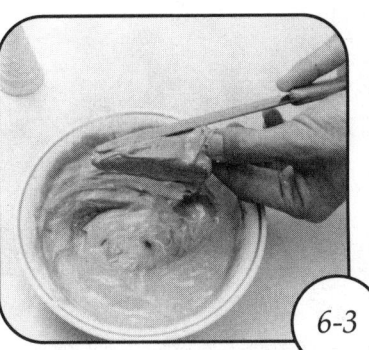

6-3

After the cone is frosted, lay the side of your knife flat on the tree and pull straight out (Figure 6-3).

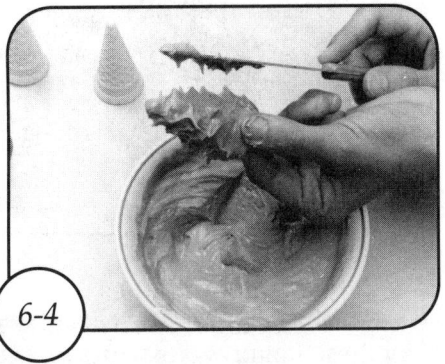

6-4

This will give you little branches (Figure 6-4).

6-5

Next hold the tree over the sink and sprinkle it with decorations (Figure 6-5). Cute, huh? Set these aside on wax paper.

WINDOWS AND SHUTTERS

You need to make four windows and four sets of shutters. For
this you will need: 4 Peppermint candies
                      8 Chocolate pieces
                  20 Red cinnamon candies

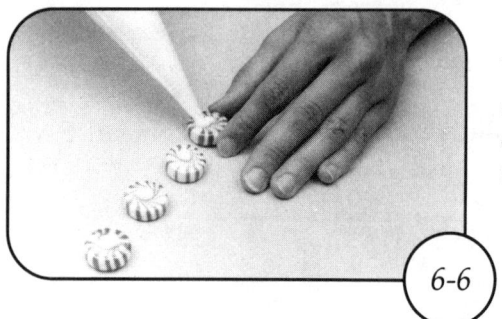

6-6

Unwrap your peppermint
candies and apply a small
dot of icing in the center
(Figure 6-6).

Next put a red cinnamon
candy on top of the icing
dot (Figure 6-7).

6-7

Do this for all four windows, and set them on the wax paper to dry.

For the shutters, break a chocolate bar apart into eight sections.
Lay these flat on your work surface.

6-7

Put a small dot of icing at
the bottom of each
chocolate piece
(Figure 6-8).

Next put a small, red cinnamon candy on top of each dot of candy (Figure 6-9).

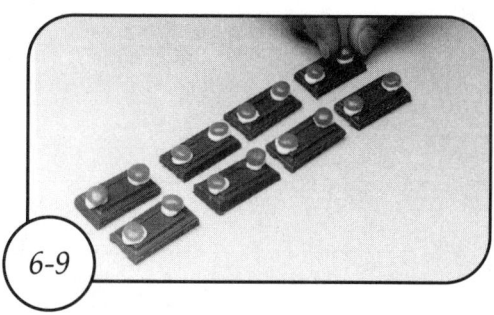

6-9

There, your windows and shutters are finished. Easy so far! Set these aside on the wax paper also.

WREATH

You will need:
1 Round jelly ring
Lifesavers
Fruit sheet

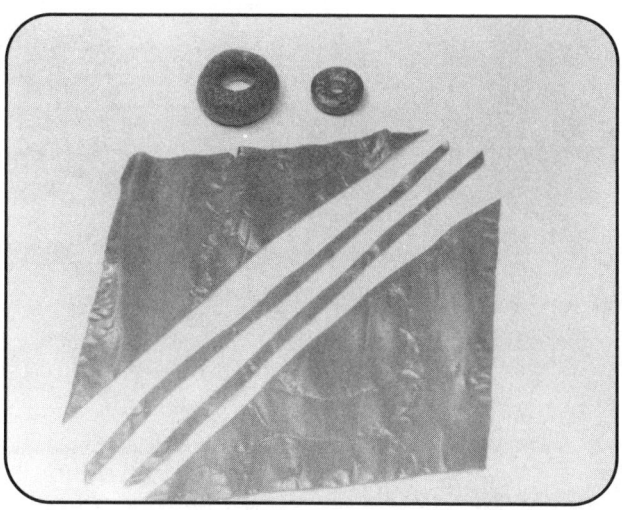

Set the jelly ring and one Lifesaver in front of you. Make your bows by cutting your fruit sheet into strips diagonally to give you a longer piece (Figure 6-10).

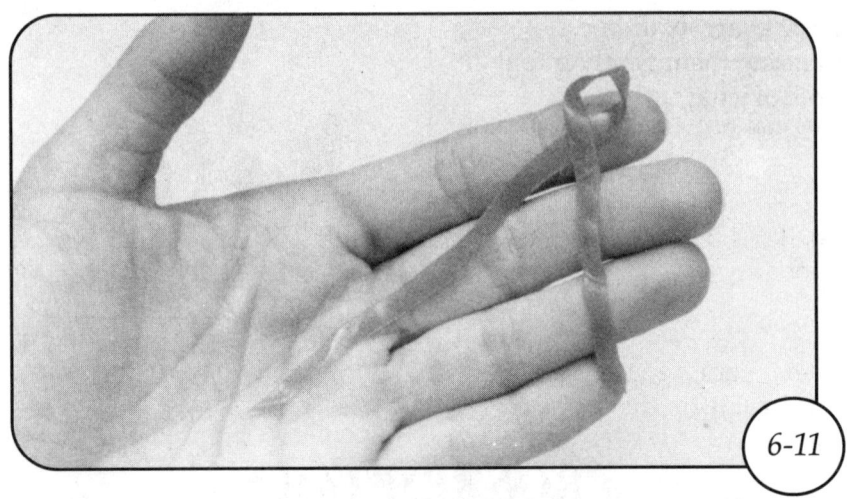

6-11

Fold into a bow by folding one side over and pressing in the center (Figure 6-11).

Then take the other side and fold it over (Figure 6-12).
Press the bow together in the center.

Make two bows, one slightly smaller than the other.

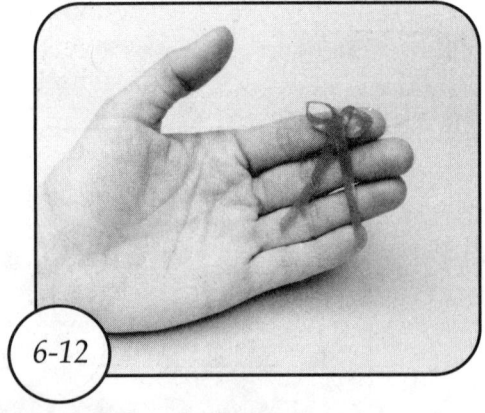

6-12

6-13

Cut the bottom of the bow as you desire.

Put a small dot of icing on the bottom of your jelly ring and a smaller dot of icing on your Lifesaver (Figure 6-13).

Now attach your bows by pressing them gently into the dots of icing
 (Figure 6-14).

6-14

Set these aside on the wax paper.

FRONT DETAILS

Here we go. Are you ready?

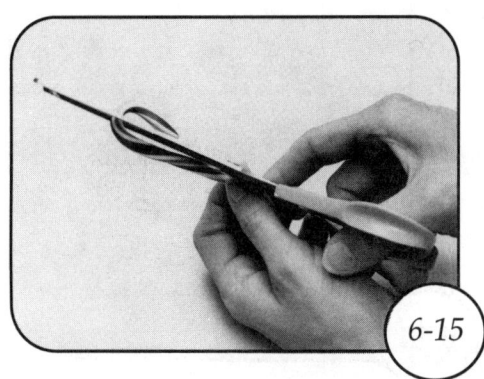
6-15

To make the front door archway, you need to cut a candy cane with scissors at the beginning of the curl (Figure 6-15).

Cut a second candy cane in the same manner (Figure 6-16).

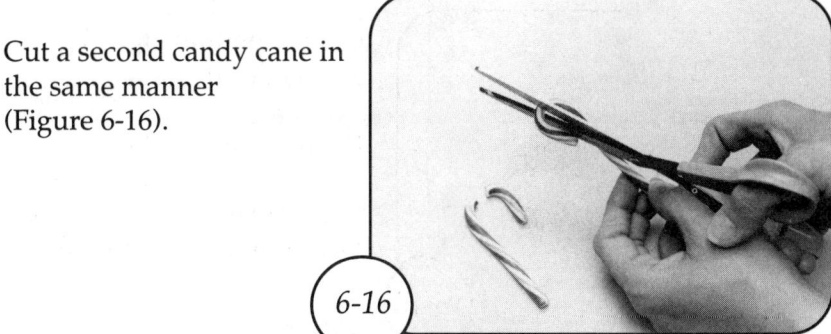
6-16

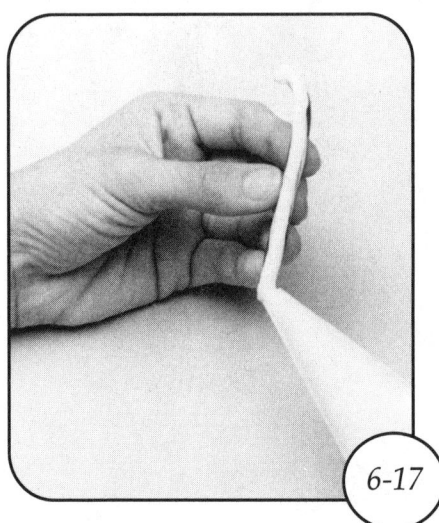

Apply a bead of icing along the back (the side that will touch the house) of the left candy cane (Figure 6-17).

6-17

Press this just off center of the front of the house (Figure 6-18). Do the same for the right side of the archway.

6-18

Leave a little space between the two candy cane pieces (Figures 6-19).

6-19

Place a jelly bean in the space that you left (Figure 6-20).

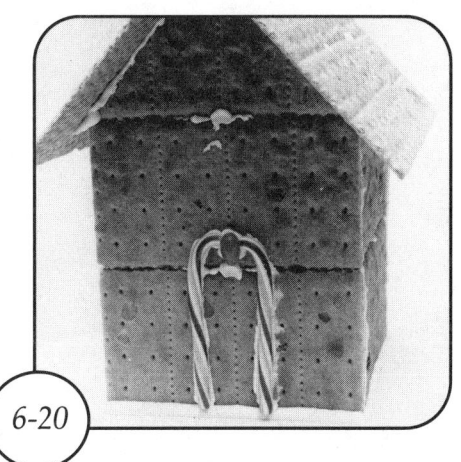

6-20

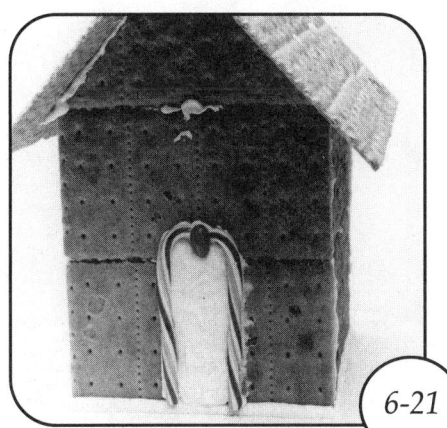

6-21

Now fill in the archway with icing. You don't have to worry about smoothing this icing out; it will look just fine (Figure 6-21).

Take the Lifesaver wreath that you made before; and, while the icing is fresh, press the wreath into the icing, placing it as you would a wreath on a real door (Figure 6-22).

6-22

6-23

At this point, if you would like to, you can decorate further with little dots of icing (Figure 6-23). You should decide now if you want to add this decoration to your house. It is easier to do after each step than it is to add it on later.

Now use a red cinnamon candy as a doorknob (Figure 6-24).

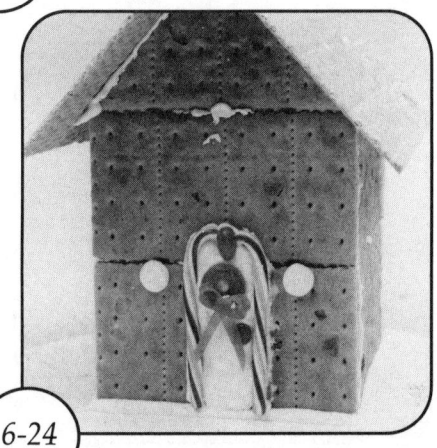

6-24

You need lights now so that your little guests don't trip on their way in. Place two dots of icing on either side of the front door, then press two yellow gumdrops on top of the icing dots (Figure 6-25).

6-25

Run a 1" bead of icing just next to the front door on both sides (Figure 6-26).

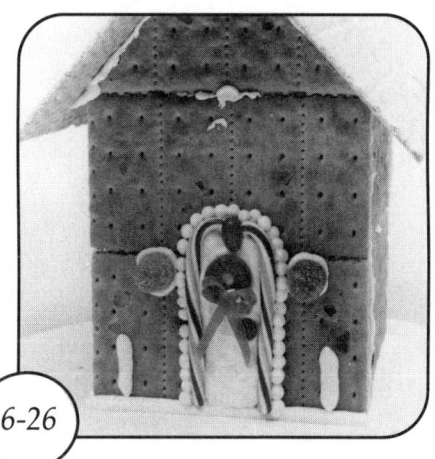

6-26

Press two pretzel men in place (Figure 6-27).

6-27

For the window above the front door, put a dot of icing approximately 2" below the peak of the roof (Figure 6-28).

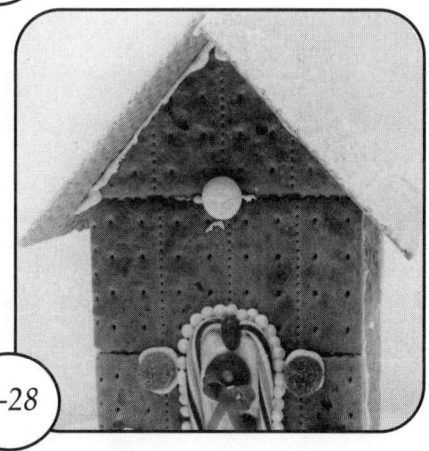

6-28

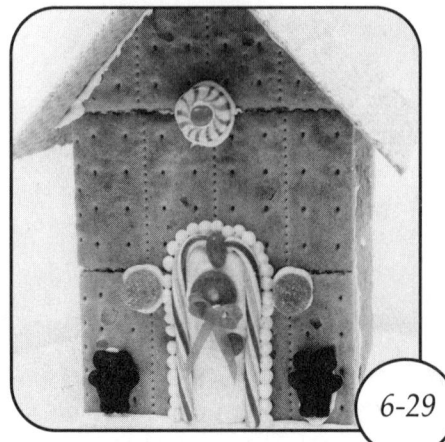

6-29

Put your peppermint window on this dot of icing (Figure 6-29).

Next to your window, run a 1" bead of icing on both sides (Figure 6-30).

6-30

Place one shutter on each bead of icing (Figure 6-31).

6-31

There you have it. You just finished decorating the front of your Holiday Wish House. Show your friends what a nice job you did. If you are in the kitchen by yourself, make someone come in and look. This moment should not go by without a little praise!

SIDE DETAILS

You will need:
2 Peppermint windows
2 Sets of shutters
2 Pretzel men

Both sides of the house are done in the same manner and are very easy and quick to do.

Put a dot of icing on the center, horizontal seam, trying to center the icing dot on the side of the house (Figure 6-32).

6-32

Place a peppermint window on this icing dot (Figure 6-33).

6-33

6-34

Run two 1" beads of icing along both sides of the window (Figure 6-34).

Place your shutters here (Figure 6-35).
Run a 1" bead of icing at both ends of the side of the house and press a pretzel man in place here (Figures 6-36 and 6-37). Your pretzel men will not fit flush to your base because the bead of icing that you ran before has dried now and is hard. That is okay. When you put your yard in, it will look just fine.

6-35

6-36

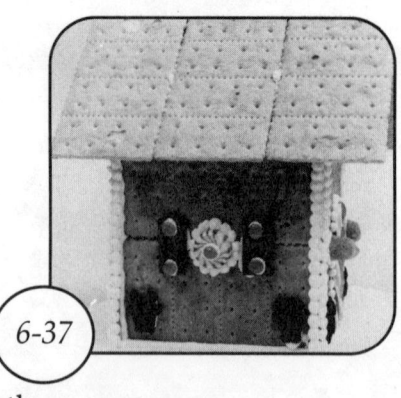

6-37

Do the second side in the same manner.

BACK DETAILS

You will need:
1 Jelly-ring wreath
1 Set of shutters
1 Peppermint window
2 Pretzel men

Put a window and a set of window shutters on the center of the horizontal back seam, using the same procedure that you used for all of the previous windows and shutters.

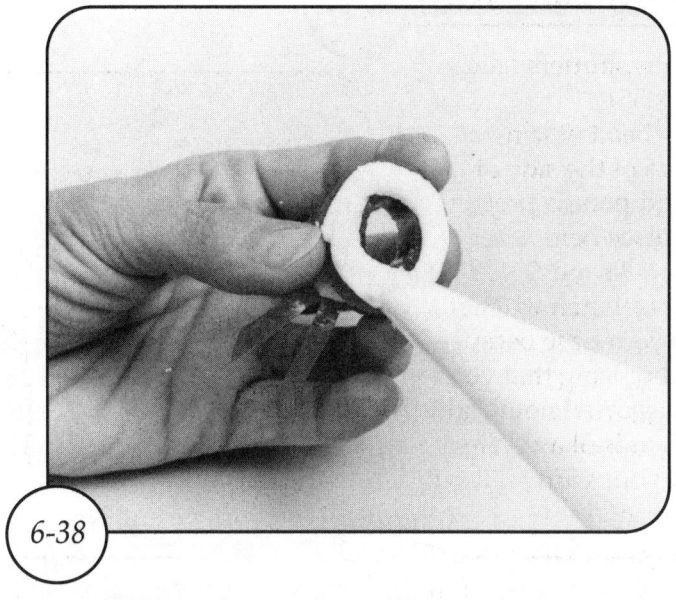

6-38

Now get the large jelly-ring wreath that you made before and run a bead of icing along the back (Figure 6-38).

Press this in place, centering it on the upper horizontal seam.

6-39

Run two 1" beads of icing along each side of the house and press a pretzel man on top of each bead (Figure 6-39).

Now the body of your house is complete. What do you think? Pretty nice job so far. Let's go on to the roof.

Before you go on to build the roof, you have the option of whether or not to finish the corners of your house. I prefer to finish mine, but it is not necessary.

Run a bead of icing along one corner of your house from where the roof meets the side to the base.

Place a small candy cane directly on top of the icing, with the curl facing out, and press in place.

Place small icing dots along the front edge beside the candy cane from the base to the peak of the roof. It makes a nice finishing touch, don't you think so too?

ROOF

The roof is very easy to do, but, for some reason, people seem to get nervous when it is time to do it. You do have to be a little more careful decorating the roof than any other place on the house. The two center seams on both sides of the roof (1) and the roof tips (2) are the weakest parts of the roof.

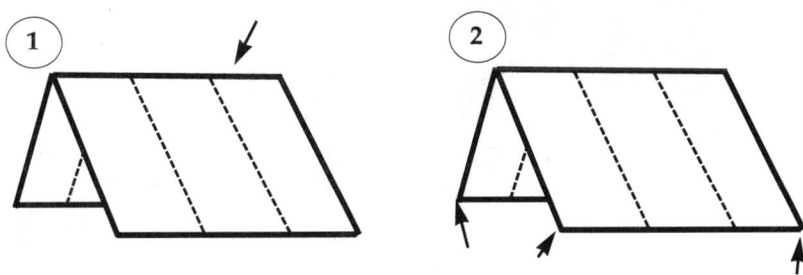

If something breaks, there are ways to correct it, so let's take a little time right now to discuss corrections.

If (and let's hope that this never happens) the center of your roof caves in, don't get too upset. Just stand back, take a deep breath and remember that it isn't the end of the world, just the end of that roof. You can try to remove the damaged side by running a sharp knife along the dried icing lines to loosen the roof and then gently lifting it off. If that doesn't seem to work for you (and you are starting to get even more nervous), try tapping it with the handle of a table knife. You can break it off bit by bit and replace it with a new roof.

If the roof end tips break off (and this has happened to me on a number of occasions), they are easily fixed. Just follow the instructions as given under item 20, Chapter 1.

6-40

Now for the decorating. Choose one side on which to start. Starting at the peak of the roof, run a bead of icing in a zigzag fashion up and down in about 1" strokes all along the front edge, bottom edge and back edge of the side on which you are working. These will be icicles that hang down (Figure 6-40).

Starting in the upper left-hand corner of the roof along the peak, run a continuous bead of icing in a long, zigzag motion from left to right all along the roof surface, finishing along the bottom edge of the roof (Figure 6-41).

6-41

6-42

Try to make the icing touch itself as you pass from one zigzag to another. This will eliminate the need to smooth the icing out with a knife later on. When you press the candies into place, it will push the icing out and smooth it (Figure 6-42).

Now take the gumdrops and gently press them into place, starting at the upper left-hand corner, going across to the right and continuing all the way down (Figures 6-43).

6-43

6-44

Do the other side of the roof in the same manner. Start with the icicles first, then fill the roof in with icing, and place your candies (Figure 6-44).

Do not try to ice both sides of the roof at one time. When you do it that way and have placed the candies on the first side, the icing has started to crust over and the candies won't stick as well by the time that you get to the second side (Figure 45).

6-45

Now run a bead of icing along the peak of the house. It is okay if you run over the gumdrops a little (Figure 6-46).

6-46

Press in two candy canes and one gumdrop in the center (Figures 6-47 and 6-48); or, if you like, you can run another row of gumdrops all along the peak.

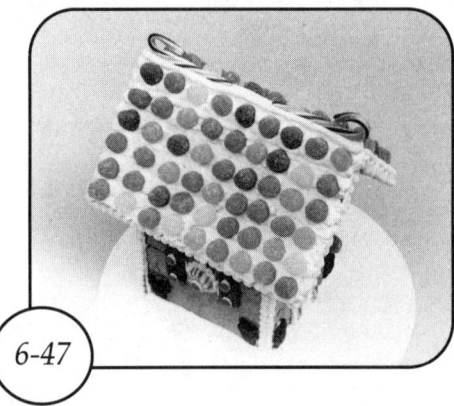

6-47

6-48

Be patient and be gentle. There you go! What do you think? Pretty good job, isn't it?
Okay, go get your family again. It is time for a little more praise. You have done a terrific job.

YARD

Kids love to decorate the yard the most. But it is important that they follow the instructions and wait until the rest of the house is decorated to do the yard. First clean off any wrappers or icing that has fallen on the base. I have chosen a very simple yard for this house. You may add any other items you wish, such as benches with gifts, sleds, reindeer, etc. Let your imagination run away with you. (If you are short on imagination, look in the back of this book for more ideas.)

Do the front section of the yard first by squeezing icing directly onto the base (Figure 6-49). You can make it look like swirls of snow by making tiny zigzag motions as you squeeze. If you prefer a smoother look to your snow, just squeeze it out and smooth it with a knife.

6-49

6-50

You may want to practice on a cookie sheet to see what effect you like better.

Add your pathway by placing jelly beans in the icing. I like a little curve to mine to add interest (Figure 6-50).

6-51

Place some of the trees that you made ahead of time at each corner (Figure 6-51).

You may want to add a few spearmint shrubs with M&M's® on top to add color (Figure 6-52).

6-52

Fill one side of the base with icing, as you did the front and place spearmint leaf shrubs and small gumdrops in the yard (Figure 6-53).
Do the other side in the same manner.

6-53

Since I placed the house close to the back of the base, there isn't much room for decorating. You can just squeeze in three gumdrops for a little color (Figure 6-54).

6-54

There you have it: your first official Holiday Wish House.

Pretty proud of yourself, aren't you? I'm sure that by now you already have an audience and don't have to call anyone to praise your beautiful work. Just smile real big, say, "it was nothing," and ask who would like to help you clean up.

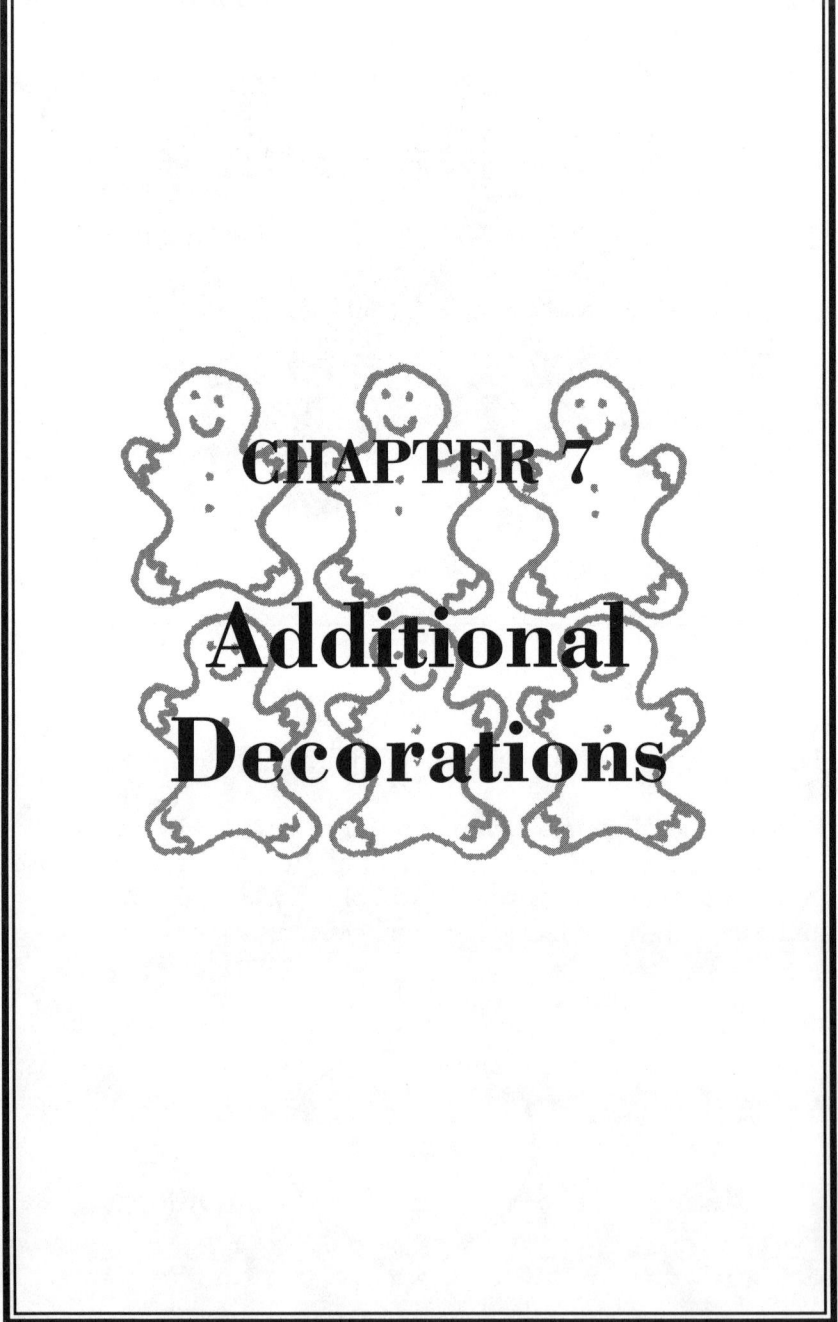

CHAPTER 7

Additional Decorations

Additional Suggestions on Decorating

The possibilities are endless. All that you need is a little imagination and away you go. It is fun to get together with some of your friends and have a Holiday Wish House Party. The time goes quickly. You have lots of fun and you also have a chance to share ideas with each other.

Here are just a few...

CHRISTMAS TREES

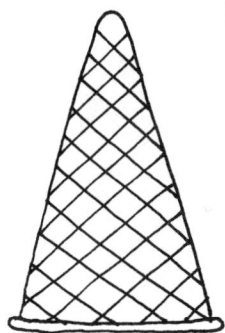

Large and small ice cream cones turned upside down make great trees. Frost with green-tinted icing, tap the iced tree with the edge of a butter knife to form branches, and then sprinkle with cake-decorator candy.

SHRUBBERY

Spearmint leaves look nice as little shrubs. With a cinnamon candy on top, they look especially festive.

Try stacking M&M's on top of each other to build your own shrubbery.

Three small gumdrops placed next to each other with a small candy on top look very nice.

Try single large gumdrops as larger, more colorful plants.

FRONT STOOPS

Sugar wafers and sandwich cookies tend to fall apart, but vanilla wafers and flat shortbread cookies make great front stoops.

DOORWAYS

Cut a round cookie in half to crown your doorway. A Lifesaver wreath and a candy door knob help add color.

BENCHES

Two whole cookies and one cut in half make a nice bench for the yard.

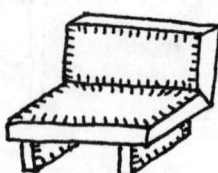

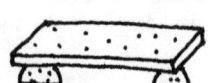

SLEDS

Sleds are created by using one whole cookie for the top and another cut in half lengthwise for the runners.

ROOF DECORATIONS

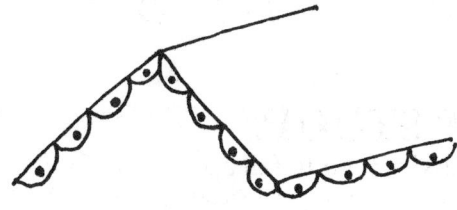

Vanilla wafers cut in half and run along the edge of the roof line make a very attractive decoration. You may also place colorful candies along the edge of the cookies.

SHUTTERS

An assortment of different shapes and designs of cookies will make very festive shutters.

FENCES

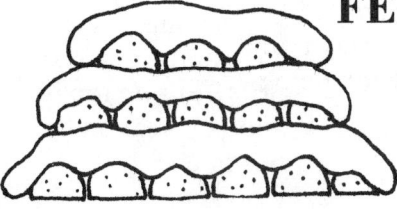

Fences always look nice in the yards. Some we have done are... Gumdrops with mortar made of magic icing.

Gumdrop and pretzel-stick split-rail fence. Push sticks gently into gumdrops with a twisting action. Attach cross rails with icing.

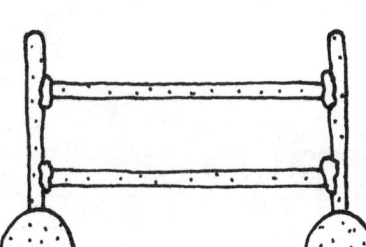

Pretzel men standing right next to each other or with a piece of square candy placed

between them seem to be a favorite with the boys, especially if they want their house to have the look of a fort or army camp. One young man even lined his front walk and top of his roof with these little guys, and it looked great.

Pretzel sticks simply lined up on top of each other make a split¬rail fence. Use dots of icing to make winter appear and help hold the fence together.

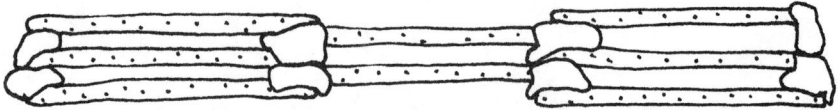

Sugar cubes and gumdrops are one of my favorites. It really gives the effect of a North Pole estate. (You know who I'm talking about, don't you?)

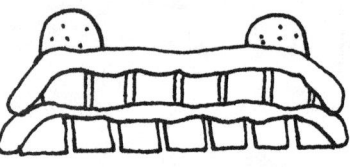

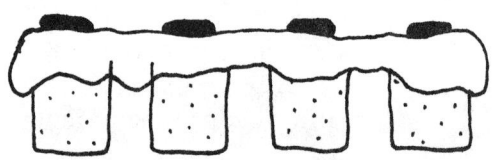

Pretzel nuggets with icing and cinnamon or M&M's on top is another creation from one of our workshops.

Small pretzels turned upside down in a patch of icing with a little icing laid on top of each pretzel look like a scene from the country. No need to go all around the house with this one. Just three or four on each side does the trick.

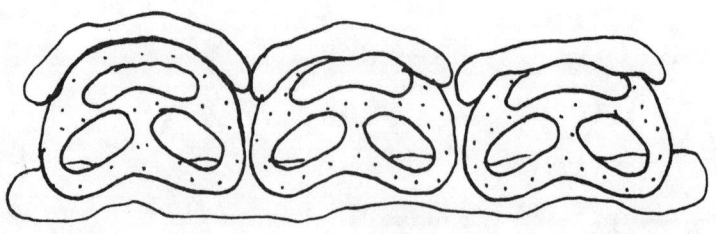

CHAPTER 8

Extras for the Yard

Extras for the Yard

GIFTS

Tiny gifts made from square pieces of colorful gum and wrapped with icing ribbons look wonderful placed on benches, in the yard or at the front door.

MARSHMALLOW SNOWMAN

With just a few ingredients you can make this adorable snowman for your front yard. All you need are 3 marshmallows, 1 gumdrop, 1 cookie wafer, 3 pretzel sticks and a few small candies for the face and buttons.

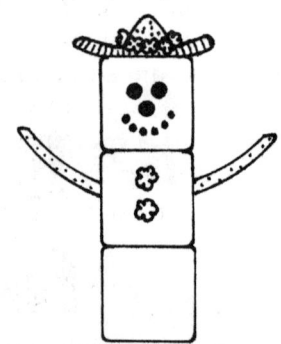

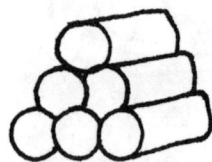

LOG PILES

Log piles can be made from licorice sticks cut in pieces, brown candy rolls or pretzel nuggets.

CAR OR SMALL TRAIN

Make one small car or a number of cars to form a little train in your yard.

MARSHMALLOW TEDDY BEAR

This may take a little more time to make, but he sure looks cute sitting on a bench with a gift next to him. All you need to make this are mini-marshmallows and tiny candies.

Cut one marshmallow in half for the ears. Use two whole marshmallows for the head and body, and cut two marshmallows in half for the arms and legs.

SKIER

This guy is my favorite! He is very simple to make. All you need is 1 pretzel man, 1 small piece of fruit roll, 1 pretzel stick and 2 candy canes cut to size.

Cut the candy canes as you did for the front of the house. Attach them to the bottom of the pretzel man with icing. Fashion a ski cap from a triangle of fruit roll and fold the top of the triangle down. Attach it to the head of the pretzel man with a dot of icing. You may have to hold this in place for a little while until it has time to set. Now break a pretzel stick in half and attach to the sides of the pretzel man with icing in the spots where you think he should be holding them.

There you have it–your own little skier. Scratch ski marks in the icing after him to make it look more realistic. If you want to add a little humor, put a hole in the snow and some icing on his backside, and see what people say!

CANDY-CANE TREES

These trees add a lot of color to the yard and also take up a lot of room. If you run short on time and candy and have a few candy-canes, gumdrops and icing left over, this will fill the yard up for you. I recommend the mini-canes for this idea.

Just attach all of the
items together with
dots of icing.

WREATHS

Wreaths can be made
from fruit rings and
Lifesavers. A bow
fashioned from a fruit
roll sheet is very nice
added touch.

REINDEER

These reindeer are cute but they take a little practice and a lot of
patience.

You will need:
1 Small pretzel
2 Pretzel nuggets
2 Pretzel sticks
1 Small red candy

You will need to cut the one small pretzel in half to form the
antlers. It took me about six tries before I finally got one that I
could use.

Cut the pretzel the same way
that you cut the candy canes.
If this does not work for you,
try gently sawing it with a
serrated knife.

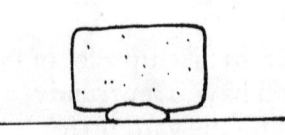

Put a small amount of icing on one of
your pretzel nuggets and stick it to your
work surface. This is going to be the
body of your reindeer. Sticking it to the
work surface allows you to work a little
more freely.

You may want to give this a little time to set. Now put a nice big dot of icing where you want the antlers to go. Push the pretzel halves into the icing and hold them in place until they take hold.

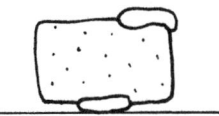

The stems of the antlers should be facing each other. You may fill small paper cups with water and place one on either side of the antlers to hold it in place so you can go on to something else.

Put a small dot of icing on another pretzel nugget, and stick it to your work surface. Now cut two pretzel sticks in half to make four legs. Put two dots of icing on both ends of the nugget andpress the little legs into the icing.

Let this dry a nice long time. You have come this far; you don't want the little guy to fall apart while you are putting him together, do you?

After it is dry, attach the body to the head with another big dot of icing where the neck would be. Make sure that you don't press too hard or you will break his legs. Ouch...

Now that his body is done and you have let him dry, he just isn't complete without a little, red nose. Use a small dot of icing and a small, red candy ball. There! Now he is finished. To make a lying deer, just omit the legs.

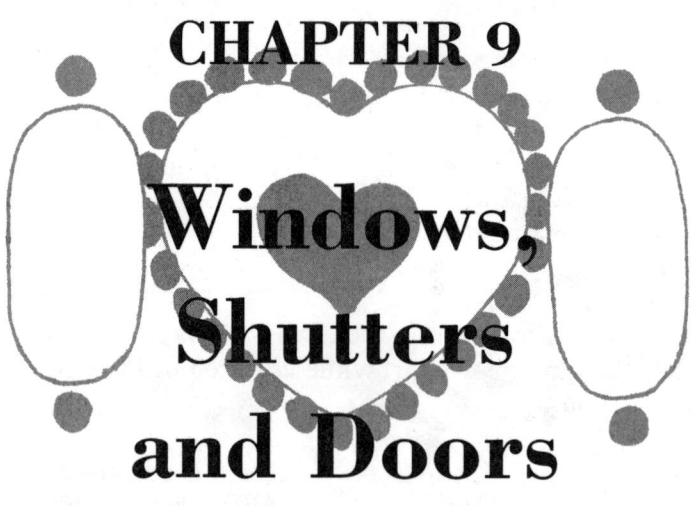

CHAPTER 9

Windows, Shutters and Doors

 # Windows, Shutters and Doors

These can be made from just about anything. Here are a few suggestions to get you started.

WINDOWS

Peppermint candies make a very nice ready-made window. Add a dot of icing in the center and a little, red cinnamon candy, and you have a very nice looking window.

 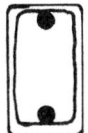

Here are some other ideas:

Large candy hearts with smaller candy hearts in the center.

Gumdrops placed next to each other or one large gumdrop shaved down to make it a little thinner.

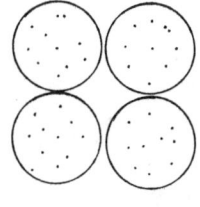 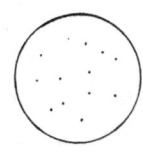

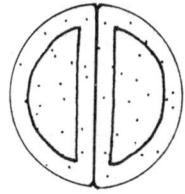

Fruit slices placed against each other to form a circle.

Lifesavers placed next to
each other.

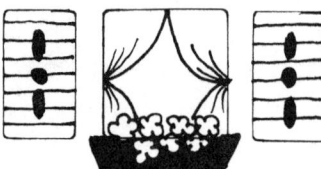

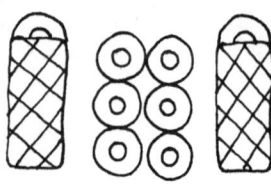

Use your icing bag and
simply outline a win-
dow. You may even put
curtains on it. Use a
piece of graham cracker
to make a window box
under it and fill it with
candy flowers.

Try a large round
Necco® wafer circled
with icing dots.

Apply a thin sugar wafer
without the icing. Place a
gumdrop on top and decorate
with tiny icing dots or candies.

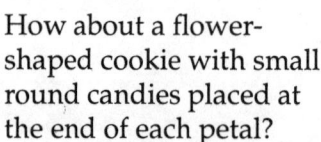

How about a flower-
shaped cookie with small
round candies placed at
the end of each petal?

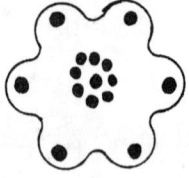

Don't be afraid to use your own imagination when it comes to
decorating these houses. I'm sure that you will be able to come
up with some wonderful ideas all on your own.

SHUTTERS

If you split a sugar wafer cookie apart and only use one thin piece with no icing, it makes a very nice cottage-type shutter. The wafers come in brown, pink, and yellow. Place small candies on them to add more color and interest.

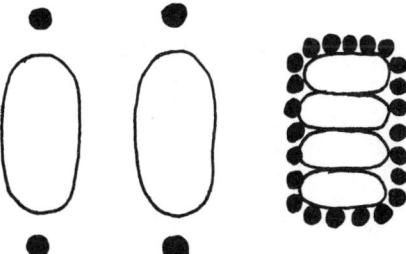

Good & Plenty® candies alone or placed close together have a very nice effect, especially if they are used with an odd-shaped window such as a heart.

Try pieces of chocolate bars decorated with colorful candies.

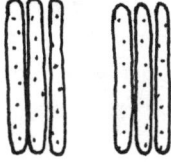

If you really want a cottage effect, try using pretzel sticks placed next to each other.

Fruit slices turned on their sides look bright and cheery.

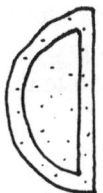 

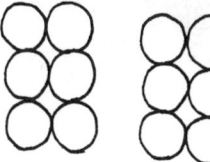

Gumdrops placed next to each other look bright and festive.

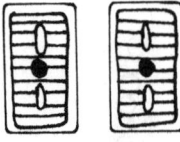

Shutters can also be created by using a wafer cookie and decorating it with icing in the design of a real shutter. Candies may also be placed on top of the icing to make them a little more colorful.

Sometimes simply placing a mini stick candy cane next to the window can create a very nice effect.

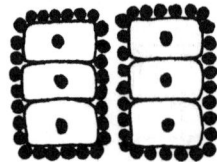

You can also use tiny squares of chewing gum decorated with small candy.

Try round candies topped with smaller candies such as M&M's or cinnamon candies. Another little addition you may like to try is simply adding dots of icing around and above the windows.

DOORS

A very simple doorway is made with M&M's and filled with icing.

Use the same idea as above, but alternate with different colors of M&M's using reds and greens.

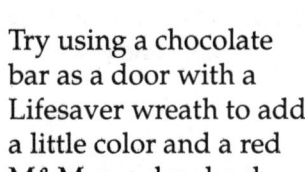

Try using a chocolate bar as a door with a Lifesaver wreath to add a little color and a red M&M as a doorknob.

Cookies make nice one-piece doors. They can be decorated with candies or left plain.

I use candy canes cut into arch ways and filled with icing on most of my houses. Put a small Lifesaver wreath on the door and a little, red doorknob for color.

CORNER DECORATIONS

The corners of the house may be decorated with candies or icing or left plain. It is a matter of personal taste.

Leaving them plain, of course, is the easiest way to do it, especially if you are doing a party for children. They may want to try their own hand at decorating the corners.

Place a candy cane at each corner for a very simple decoration. You may use a mini candy cane or a stick candy cane. The colored stick candy that you can find at any time of the year looks very nice also, especially if you try to coordinate the houses colors.

Try simply using large dots of icing up and down all of the corners. If you want to get a little fancy, place small candies at the front of each dot.

♥ ♥ ♥ ♥ ♥

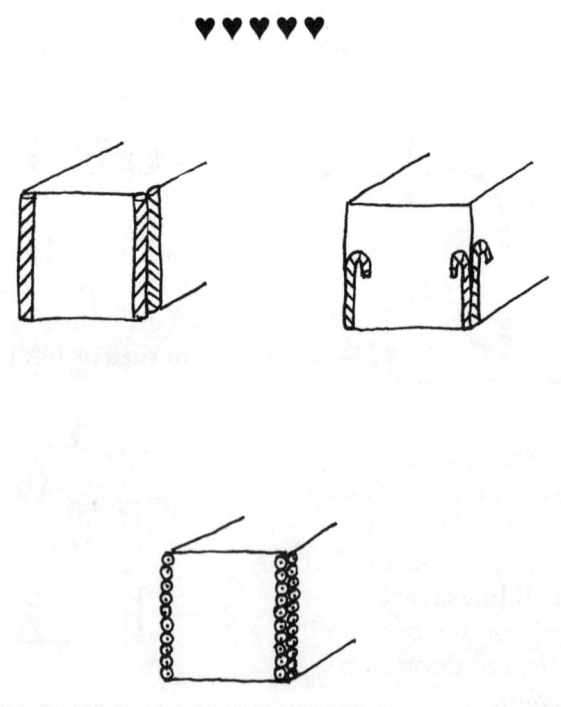

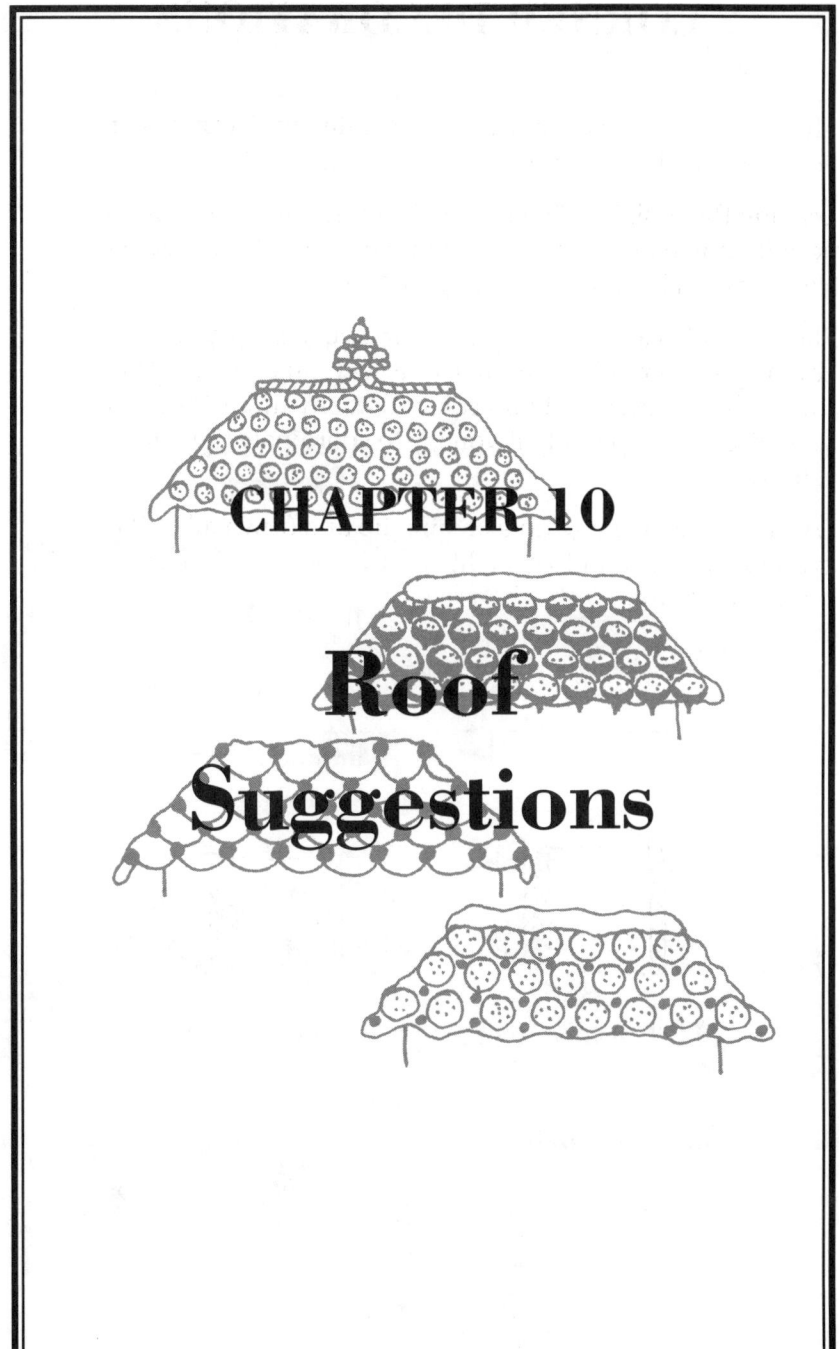

CHAPTER 10

Roof Suggestions

ROOF SUGGESTIONS

Roofs can be made from just about anything.

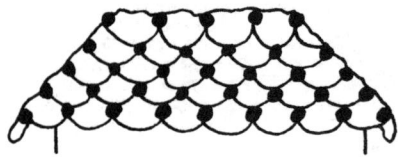

They can be very simple with only a few candies and an icing border...

...or they can be all candies with tons of icing.

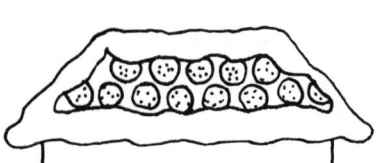

If you want it to look like it has been snowing all night long, decorate first with candy and then pipe icing all around the edges and along the peak of the roof.

You may want to try dipping your candies in a bowl of icing and then placing them on your roof.

How about topping your roof off with...

candy canes and gumdrops...

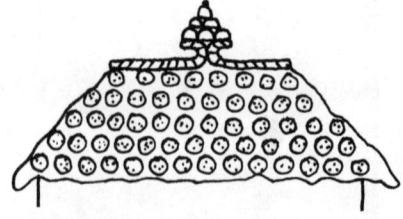

rows of candies...

gum drops and nonpareils...

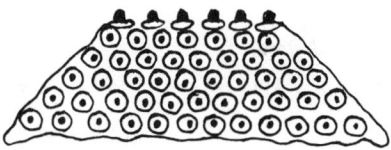

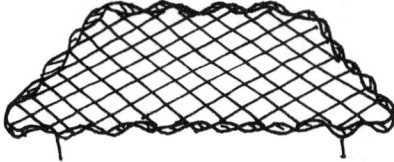

decorative edges of icing...

M&M's and jelly beans...

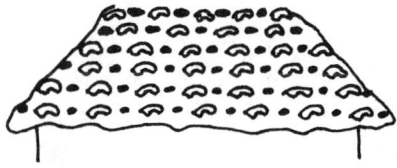

There is nothing cuter than a tiny chocolate Santa coming out of a chimney. Don't get excited. It isn't as tough as it seems.

Here are directions to make two different types of chimneys. Read them carefully first and then go on to bigger and better things.

CHIMNEY #1

You need three crackers for this chimney. Use the two extra pieces of cracker that you saved when you made the mitered roof section. These are already partially cut for you. The third cracker should be a small piece (one-forth of a whole cracker).

Place the diagonally cut extra pieces with the angle pointing to your left. Cut a small piece, about 1/2", off of the bottoms of both diagonally cut pieces. Cut about the same amount off of the third piece of cracker (Figure 10-1).

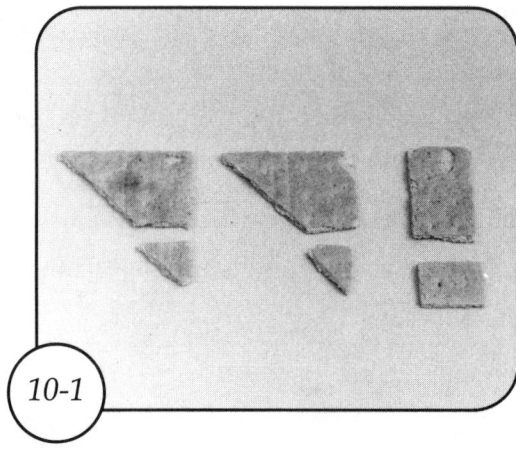

10-1

Now that your pieces are cut, you can assemble your chimney right onto your roof. You must do this before you ice your roof.

10-2

Run a bead of icing along the diagonal edge of one of your angled pieces. Place this right onto the roof where you want your chimney to be located (Figure 10-2).

Do this same procedure with the second angled piece. Remember to place the small, flat, cut side at the peak of your roof.

Now run a bead of icing along all four outside edges of the two angled pieces. Attach the longer piece to the outside of the chimney and the smaller piece to the peak side of the chimney. If you have spaces, don't worry; you may fill these in with icing if you like (Figure 10-3).

10-.3

CHIMNEY #2

For this chimney, you will need four pieces of the cracker that

you saved from the mitered roof sections and two additional small pieces of cracker (one-forth of a whole cracker) (Figure 10-4).

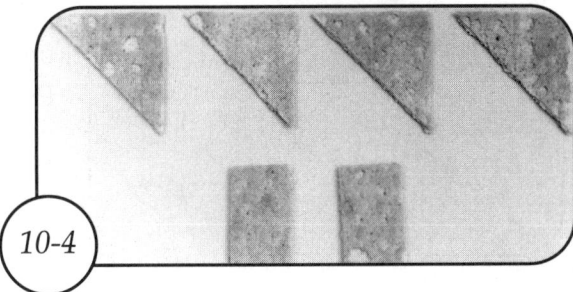

10-4

10-5

Put a small dot of icing on the inside of one of your mitered pieces. Attach this cracker to a second mitered piece to form one side of the chimney. The angles of the cracker should be facing each other.

Now adjust the crackers by sliding them up and down on each other to take the shape of the roof peak. Once you have adjusted the angle, run a bead of icing along the bottoms of both angled pieces and attach this to the roof (Figures 10-5 and 10-6).

10-6

10-7

Now run a bead of icing along the inside edge of the piece that you just attached to the roof and put both side pieces in place (Figure 10-7).

Form the back section by using the same procedure that you used to form the front section. Slide this back piece into place and run a bead of icing along all four edges to reinforce (Figure 10-8).

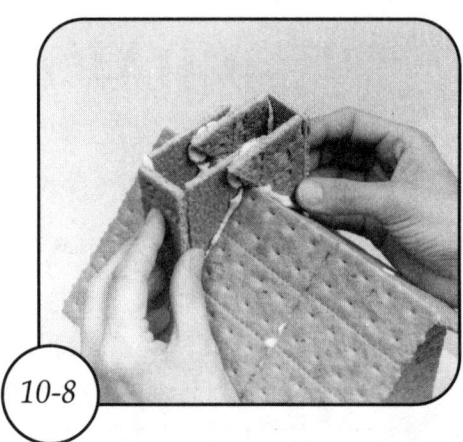

10-8

10-9

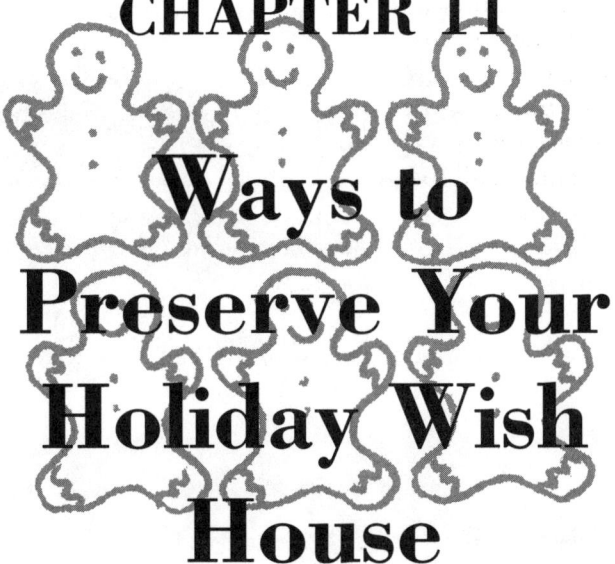

CHAPTER 11

Ways to Preserve Your Holiday Wish House

Ways to Preserve Your Holiday Wish House

FREEZING

A nice thing to do for the children is to freeze the house after the holiday season and take it out of the freezer in the summer to eat. Remember, though, that any chocolate will turn white. The children don't seem to mind the way that it looks, and it still tastes perfectly fine.

Cover the house with a paper towel, place it into a plastic freezer bag and seal the end tightly. Make sure that there are no holes in the bag so that you don't get freezer burn. Place the covered house in the freezer until you are ready to take it out. When you are ready to defrost, uncover the house, place a paper towel over the roof, and put it in the microwave oven on HIGH for one minute. ENJOY!

I recommend freezing only if the house is to be eaten in a few months. Also, do not temporarily store the house in the refrigerator during the holiday season. It is too damp, and the house will cave in.

SPRAYING

You may spray your house if you prefer. Unsprayed, it will last for about three years. It is up to you. If you want to spray your house, I suggest that you go to your nearest craft store and ask what they recommend. Make sure that your house has ample time to dry. Spray the house with a very light coat of spray, being sure to get under the roof sections. If you spray too heavily, the spray will turn yellow. After the first coat has dried completely, apply another thin second coat. Use only a recommended craft spray. **DO NOT USE HAIR SPRAY.** It will make the house turn yellow and tends to make all candies break down quickly and bleed.

STORING

Store your house in a cool, dry place–not in an attic or crawl space. Do not store in an area where it will be hit by direct sunlight. A basement corner or top of a closet is best. Just wrap your house in paper towels. This tends to catch any moisture. Place your house in a plastic bag. Poke a few air holes in the bag to let moisture escape. Tie or twist the end up nice and tight. Place the house in a box and store away. It should be fine until next year. The house itself will last up to three years. Because it is a food product, some shrinking will occur. Repairs can be made with the Magic Icing at any time.

EATING

This happens to be my family's favorite way to treat a Holiday Wish House. We just keep the house on a tabletop well out of the reach of our dog. The children break a piece off any time they want and, as the holiday season disappears, so does our house. Yes, the crackers do get stale, and the candies do get hard; but the children still think that it is a wonderful and magical holiday tradition.

CHAPTER 12

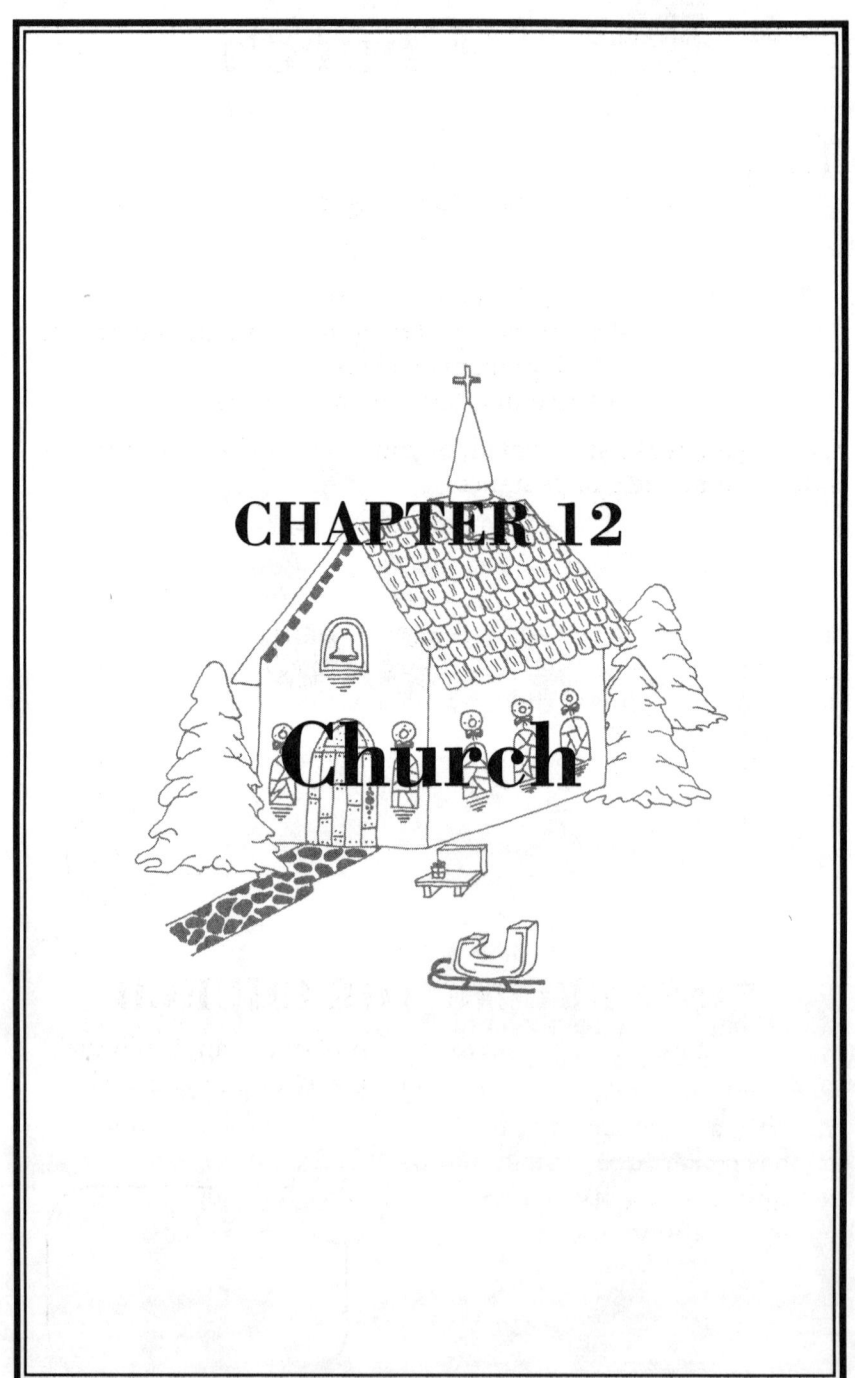

Church

Church

The basic Wish House can be converted into a "Church" very easily. All you need to do is add a steeple.

You will need:

2 Large ice cream cones
4 Scrap pieces of diagonally cut graham cracker
2 Half graham crackers
3 Three-quarter graham crackers

Once again, make sure that all of your crackers have the same side out for a nicer appearance.

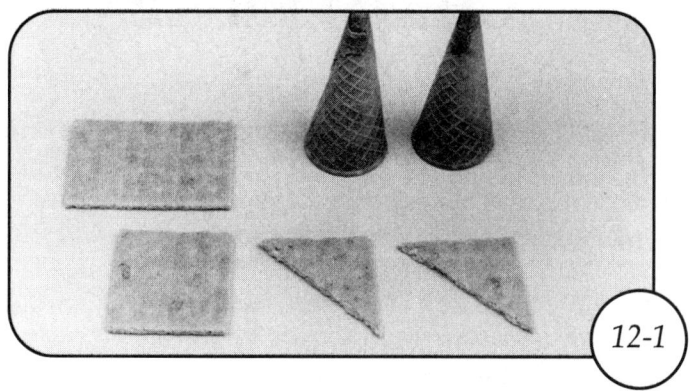

12-1

ASSEMBLING THE CHURCH

Apply a small dot of icing to the corner of one triangle (Figure 12-2) and press a second triangle into place (Figure 12-3). This will make the front.

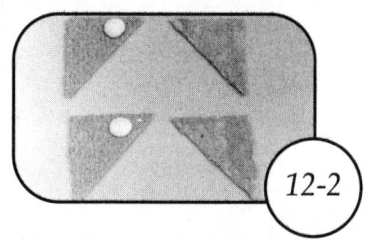

12-2

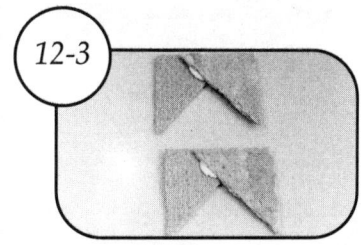

12-3

79

Now place it temporarily on the roof to adjust the angle (Figure 12-4). Do the same procedure to make the back piece (Figure 12-5).

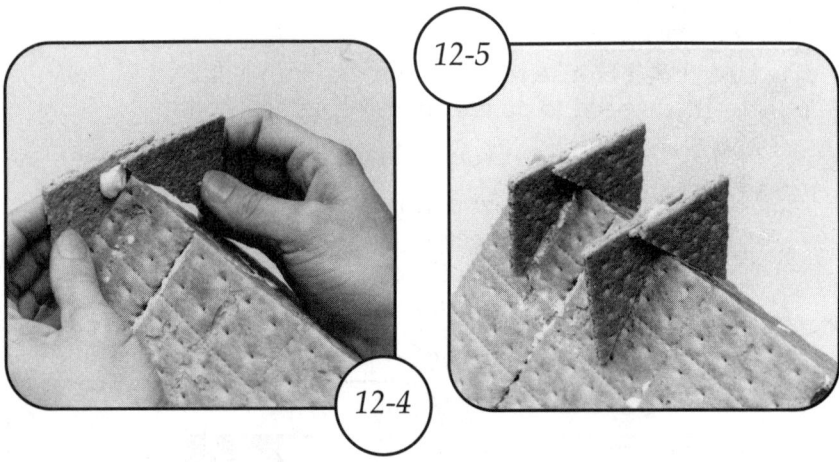

Using the half cracker as a measurement, decide where you want to place your steeple by holding it between the front and back pieces and moving it along the roof until you are pleased with the position. Anchor the back piece by running a bead of icing along the bottom edges and pressing it into place. Run a bead of icing along the right and left inside of the back piece and bottom of both side pieces.

Now press in place (Figure 12-6).

12-7

Run a bead of icing along both front side edges (Figure 12-7).

Run a bead of icing along the angled edges of the front piece and press in place (Figure 12-8). Adjust the fit and wipe off any excess icing.

12-8

12-9

You will have to cut a three-quarter cracker to fit. It will not fit evenly, but you can fill in any openings with icing and smooth it out with your fingers. Attach the top with icing (Figure 12-9).

Apply an icing dot to the pointed end of one ice cream cone and around the bottom edge (Figure 12-10) and position it on top of the steeple (Figure 12-11). Gently press the second cone onto the first (Figure 12-12) and you are all finished with your church steeple.

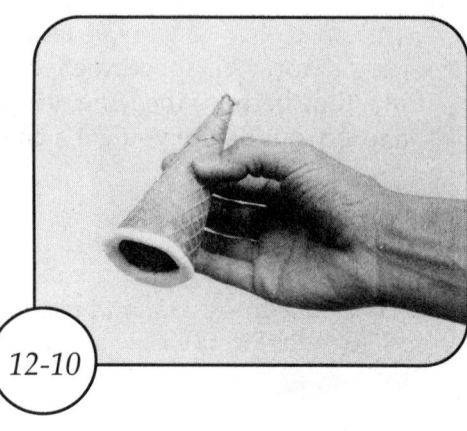

12-10

12-11

12-12

DECORATING SUGGESTIONS

There are many different ways to decorate your church. Here are a few ideas to get you started.

Body

You may leave the body of the church brown, or you could try covering it with white icing to make it look a little more country.

Just ice it as you would a cake, and then run a fork through the wet icing to form a clapboard effect. Remember to only do one side at a time because the icing will set too quickly on you and begin to dry out before you get a chance to decorate the whole way around.

Roof

I like to ice the entire roof and use red licorice squares as shingles. I also like to tuck small sugar cubes up under the roof just to add another nice little touch.

Steeple

You can either leave the steeple plain or ice it with the white icing. After I ice it, I like to add red sprinkles to match the roof. Then I add a small chocolate cross to the very top.

Windows

I like to cut fruit rolls into pieces to form stained glass windows. This works very nicely because they are easy to cut and come in many different colors.

Doors

A pink wafer cookie makes a lovely front door with a yellow gumdrop as a doorknob. A fruit slice placed above the front door gives the effect of another stained glass window.

Bell

What country church would be complete without a bell to call all of its people? You may cut the shape of the window out of a yellow fruit roll or bend red licorice into shape. Slice a bell-shaped chocolate drop or gumdrop in half and place inside the bell window.

Yard

I like to ice the entire yard, then place lots of trees and maybe a bench or two in it. A tiny, red, plastic sleigh placed next to the front door is a very nice added touch. A pathway can be made from irregular shaped candies to give the effect of a stone walkway.

If you have a cake decorating store near you, see if you can find edible crystal sprinkles. They are clear and shiny and create a beautiful effect of freshly fallen snow.

CHAPTER 13
Train

Train

Making this train can be lots of fun. All you need is the basic Magic Icing recipe and two or three boxes of graham crackers. Try the Wish House first before you try the Train. The only reason for this is that there is a lot of cutting and fitting. I don't want you to get discouraged by trying this train project first. Again, please read all directions first and gather all of your ingredients. Okay...let's get started.

ENGINE

2 Sides
1 Bottom
2 Half crackers for window sections
1 Half cracker for front of engine
1 Quarter cracker for cow catcher
1 Half cracker for top of engine
Ice cream cup for smokestack
4 Cookie wheels

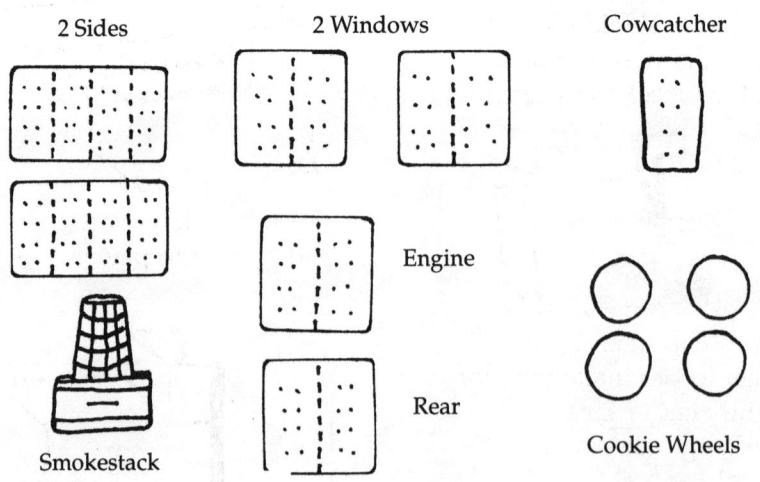

2 Sides   2 Windows   Cowcatcher

Engine

Rear

Smokestack   Cookie Wheels

Cut crackers to fit windshield back piece and roof . Attach window sections to both side sections, making sure that they are on the "inside" of the car and facing the same way. Run a bead of icing along the long bottom side and attach the side section. If you have to, lean the side section up against something to hold it for you. Apply a bead of icing to the inside right front side and bottom edge.

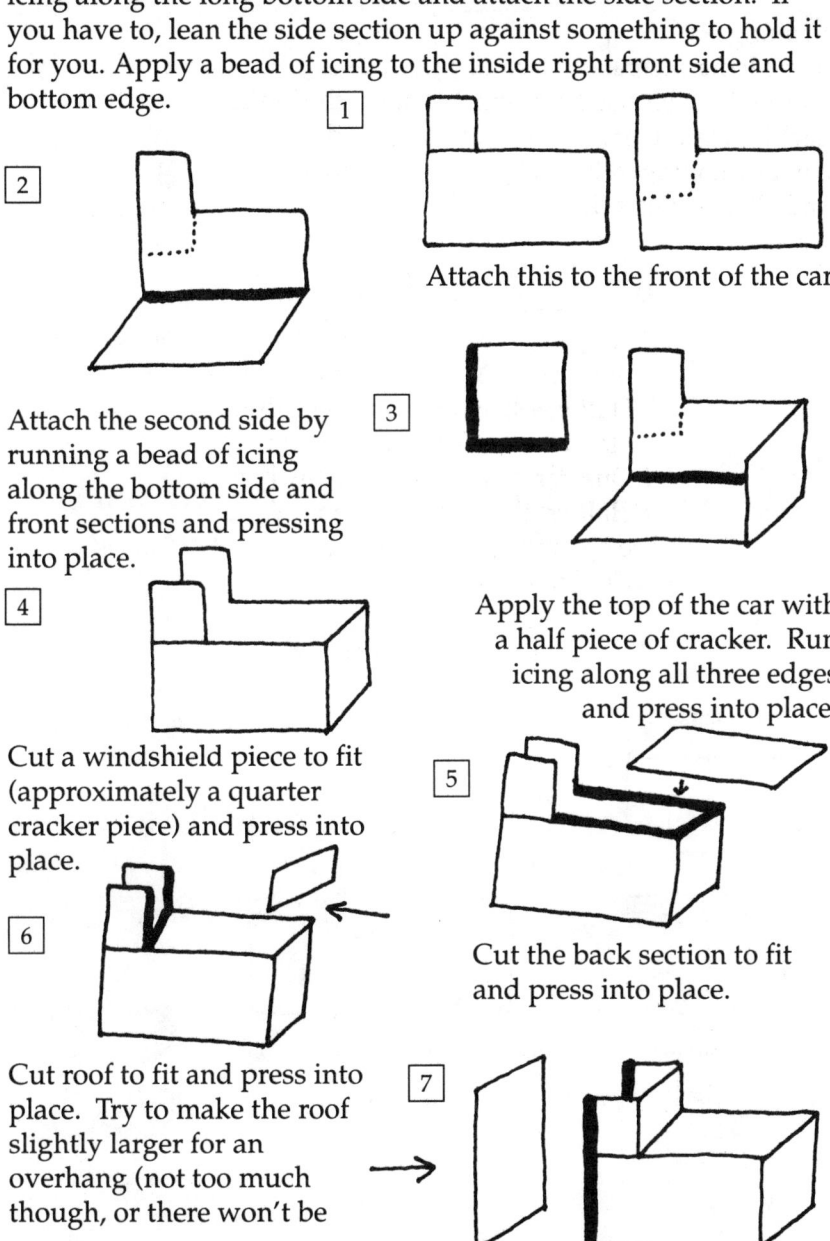

Attach this to the front of the car.

Attach the second side by running a bead of icing along the bottom side and front sections and pressing into place.

Apply the top of the car with a half piece of cracker. Run icing along all three edges and press into place.

Cut a windshield piece to fit (approximately a quarter cracker piece) and press into place.

Cut the back section to fit and press into place.

Cut roof to fit and press into place. Try to make the roof slightly larger for an overhang (not too much though, or there won't be enough room for the smokestack.)

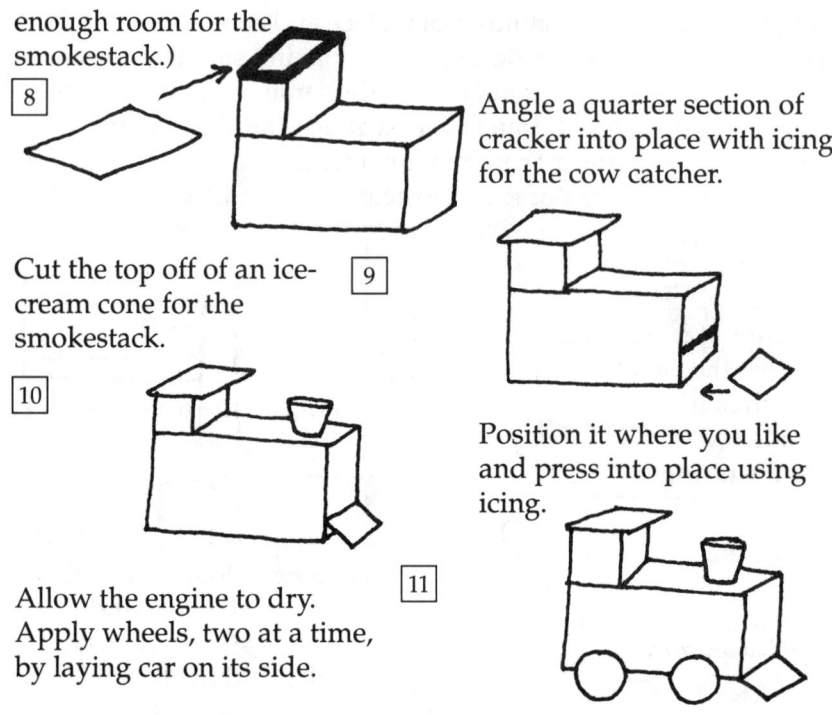

Angle a quarter section of cracker into place with icing for the cow catcher.

Cut the top off of an ice-cream cone for the smokestack.

Position it where you like and press into place using icing.

Allow the engine to dry. Apply wheels, two at a time, by laying car on its side.

COAL CARS

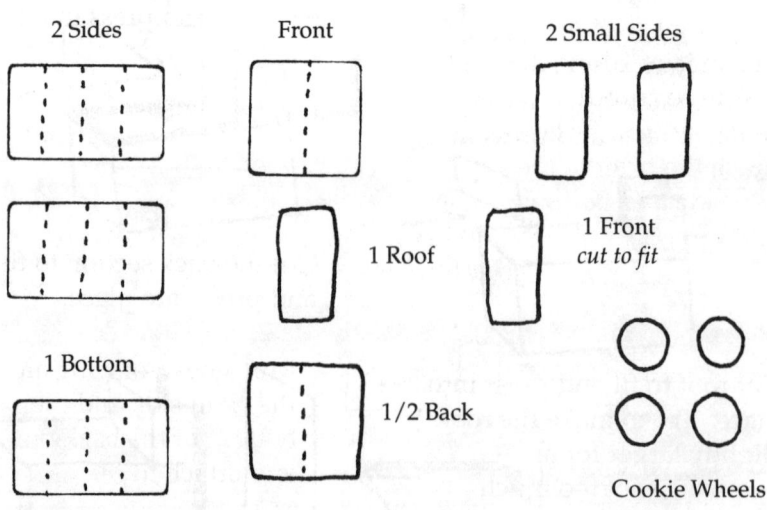

2 Sides

Front

2 Small Sides

1 Roof

1 Front
cut to fit

1 Bottom

1/2 Back

Cookie Wheels

1 Bottom piece
2 Side pieces
2 Small side pieces
1 Small roof piece
1 Front piece cut to fit
4 Cookie wheels
1 Half cracker for back

Attach two small pieces to both side pieces with a small dot of icing. Make sure that the small pieces are both on the inside of the side sections and that both are facing front.

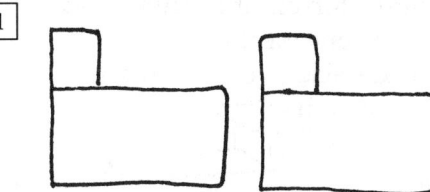

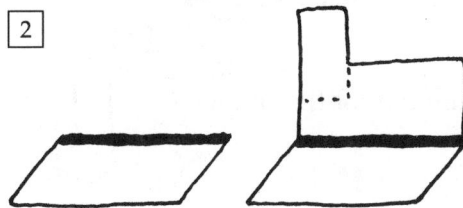

Run a bead of icing along the right long side of the bottom cracker. (If the icing is stiff, the cracker will stand by itself.) Attach the right side.

Run a bead of icing along the right side and bottom of the front section. Do not run icing along the outside edge, but run it on the flat side of the cracker. Attach the front to the right side and bottom.

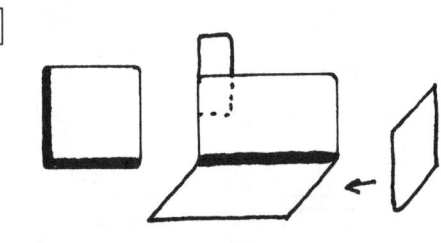

NOTE: *The side pieces will be a little higher than the front and back pieces. This can be covered later with icing.*

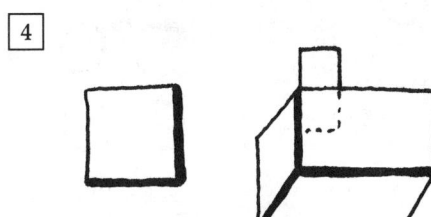

Run a bead of icing along the right side and the bottom of the back piece and attach to car.

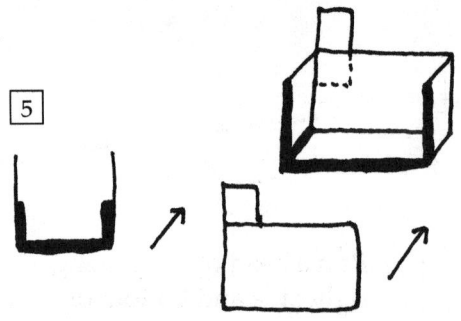

5

Run a bead of icing along the inside of the front piece, the long bottom piece and the back piece. It should look like a wide U.

Gently slide the remaining side piece into place. If your crackers slide, gently realign them. Let dry.

6

Run a bead of icing along the front edge and upper side pieces. Attach small roof piece.

7

Attach four cookie wheels as you did for the engine.

BOX CARS

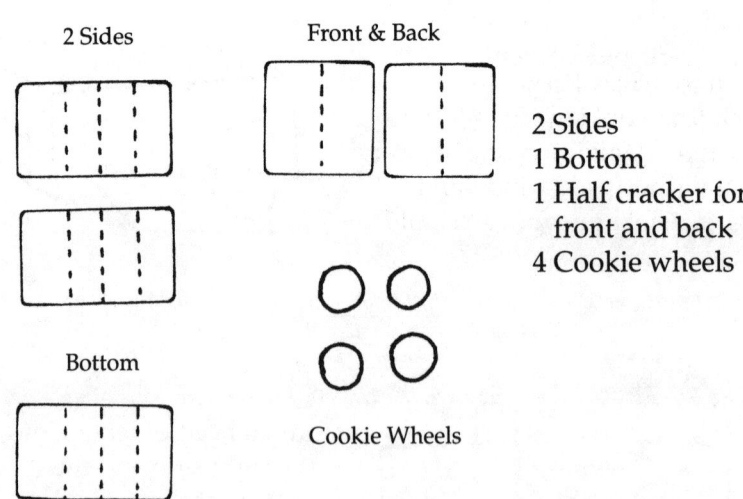

2 Sides

Front & Back

Bottom

Cookie Wheels

2 Sides
1 Bottom
1 Half cracker for front and back
4 Cookie wheels

Run a bead of icing along the long side of the bottom cracker and attach it to the right side.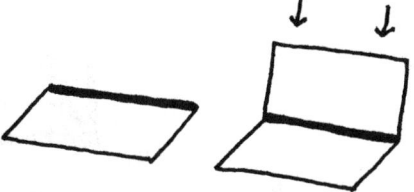

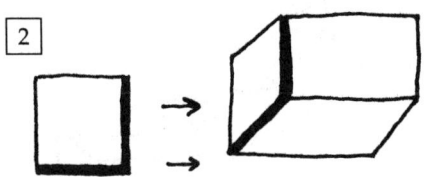 Run a bead of icing along the right side and bottom of the front section. Attach the front to the right side and bottom.

Run a bead of icing along the right side and the bottom side of the back piece and attach back to car.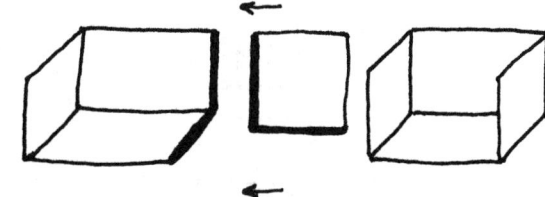

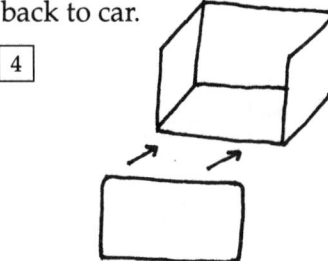 Run a bead of icing along the inside of the front piece, the long bottom piece and the back piece. It should look like a wide **U**.

Gently slide the remaining side piece into place. Let dry. Attach four cookie wheels as you did before. Make as many box cars as you wish to hold candy and treats, possibly one for each child personalized with the name.

CABOOSE

1 Bottom
1 Top
2 Half crackers for the front and back
1 Quarter cracker cut in half
1 Quarter cracker cut in half then two
1 Quarter cracker for roof

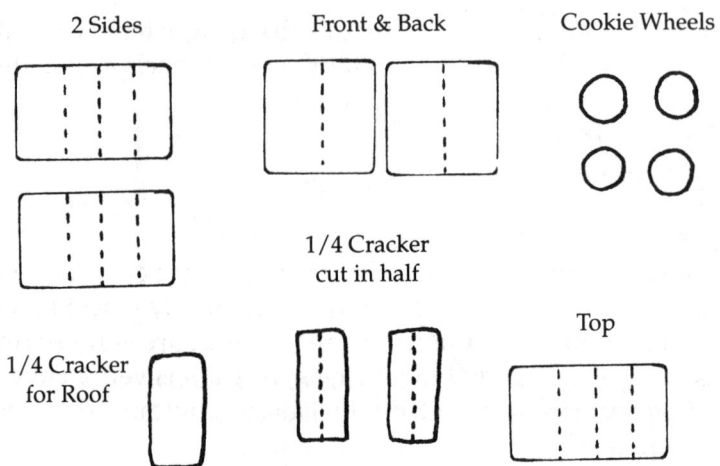

2 Sides   Front & Back   Cookie Wheels

1/4 Cracker
cut in half

1/4 Cracker
for Roof   Top

Follow boxcar directions to make the basic box.
After you have the basic box completed, run a bead of icing
along all four upper edges and gently press the top section into
place.

1

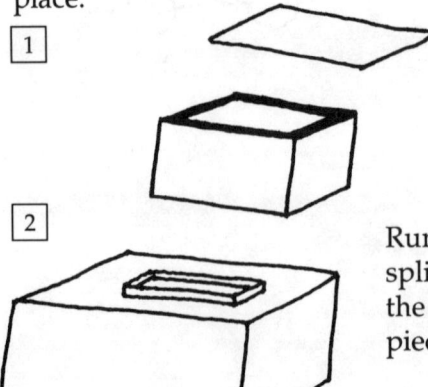

2

Run a bead of icing along one of the
split quarter pieces and press it onto
the top section. Follow with all four
pieces to form the roof section.

Run a bead of icing along all four
upper edges of the roof sections and
apply the small rooftop.

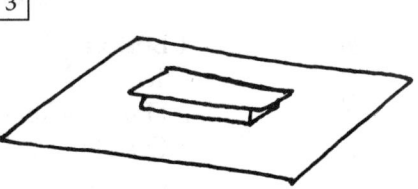

4

Let this dry completely. Then attach
all four cookie wheels as you did
before.

Now the only thing that is missing is all of your beautiful decorations. You can display the train by either simply placing it on a
table top or mounting it on cardboard. Make sure you use two
pieces of cardboard glued together, as the train is very heavy
when it is decorated and filled with candy. You can add trees, a
track, snowmen...anything you can think of.
You may also use this idea for a child's birthday. Make one
boxcar for each child and put his or her name on it. Children feel
extra special when they get to take their own train car home.

CHAPTER 14

Other Holiday Houses

Other Holiday Houses

HAUNTED MANSION

We have a lot of fun trying to think of different things to use to decorate this unusual "Haunted Mansion."

Try building this house with cinnamon crackers. They are darker in color and have more of a texture to them. You may also want to tint your icing. That way, it will not be so clean and white looking. After all, who ever heard of a clean haunted mansion?

Windows

For the windows, we used pieces of brown licorice cut into pieces to form the window frames. You may also use broken cookies or pieces of shredded wheat.

Shutters

We used broken pieces of sugar wafer cookies. We even placed one in the yard under the window to look as if it fell off of the house. If you can find a small plastic hand, it looks very scary coming out of one of the windows.

Doors

The front door was made from a cookie that we beat up a little bit with the tip of a knife. Again, we added a licorice window and a crumbly old doorknob.

Steps

Of course, what haunted mansion would be complete without a pair of rickety old steps just waiting to be tripped over? We cracked some extra graham crackers and just set them in front. If you can find a plastic spider, you may want to put it somewhere in front of the house so people will be sure to see it.

Spider Webs

Of course, if you have spiders, you must have spider webs. This is very easily done by using cotton candy. Just pull on it lightly and set it in place. Make sure that you hands are very dry when you are working with the cotton candy or it will melt. Also, only use the candy when the house is completed and all of the icing is dry.

Tombstones

We have to have a couple of tombstones in the yard. Use icing to write on a cookie cut in half and place it in the yard on a bed of puffy icing.

Signs

Make a few "Keep out!" and "Stay Away!" signs using paper taped onto toothpicks.

Fence

If all of that doesn't keep people away, make a fence out of chocolate bars. You can cut a point on the ends of each piece. Don't worry about breaking the chocolate; it adds to the effect.

Witch

If you are lucky enough to find a chocolate witch just the right size, she will look wonderful in the yard or peeking out from around the back of the house.

PILGRIM'S PLACE

If you would like to try something different with this house, do this. Build the basic Wish House as your did before, but do not put the roof on. Let the square body of the house dry and apply pretzel sticks all over the outside of the house. Allow these to dry, trim any excess pretzels away from the top edge and then put the roof on.

Roof

A nice roof for Thanksgiving, whether you use the log cabin look or not, is Shredded Wheat® cereal. It makes the roof look thatched.

Chimney

Most Pilgrims needed to be warm, so a chimney is a very nice touch. We placed light and dark brown M&M's to make it look like a stone chimney. A little cotton candy can give the effect of smoke rising out of the chimney.

Windows

We simply outlined a window with an icing bag, then added curtains and small pretzel sticks as shutters.

Door

A quarter section of a graham cracker makes a nice door for the front of your house. It looks very rustic and weather beaten. Add a brown M&M and a small "Welcome" sign over the door, and it will look very inviting.

Pathway

We like to use light and dark brown M&M's as our pathway. It looks very nice, and it also matches the chimney.

Yard

Here you can become very creative. A nice, little, log pile next to the house adds a little bit of warmth to the entire scene. A large Tootsie Roll® cut and placed on its end looks like an old tree stump just waiting to be sat upon.

You may want to try a garden. Spread some icing on your base and then sprinkle it with brown sugar to give the effect of dirt. Place in it the Thanksgiving candies that you find in any grocery store: corn, pumpkins, etc. You may be lucky enough to find a foil-covered, plump little Pilgrim to place next to the front door just waiting to welcome his guests for a Thanksgiving feast. Remember to tint your icing to fit the season.

SWEETHEART SPECIAL

What nicer gift to give your sweetheart on Valentine's Day than this beautiful "Sweetheart Special"? This is no different than any of the other houses in this book, except that we like to keep all of the colors pink, red, and white. This helps to carry the theme of Valentine's Day a little further. One other nice idea you may want to try is, before you put the roof on the house, why not slip a small gift inside the house? What a nice added surprise for that someone special!

Roof

We iced the roof with icing tinted a pale pink and added pink hearts and red cinnamon candies.

Chimney

A small chimney iced with white icing, dotted with red, cinnamon candies and heart-shaped suckers coming from inside looks very nice.

Windows

We chose to pipe the windows on the house with our decorator tube. This way, we were able to add curtains and tiny dots just about anywhere we wanted.

Window box

A window box was made from small cookies and attached to the side of the house with icing. After it was dry, we placed candy flowers inside.

Door

The door is a pink, sugar wafer with a small heart and cinnamon candy as a doorknob.

Around the door and on both sides of the house, we placed many tiny hearts surrounded with tiny icing dots.

Pathway

Our pathway is very simply a white icing path surrounded on both sides with pretty pink and white candies. You may also sprinkle pink and white candy flowers on the path if you like. These would also match the flowers in the window boxes.

Yard

In our yard, we have a bench made from red and white ribbon candy placed on top of two red and white candy mints. Placed on top of the bench is, of course, a gift for the sweetheart. We also made a special, tiny garden overflowing with chocolate kisses and candy flowers.

EASTER COTTAGE

You may want to try to build your "Easter (or Spring) Cottage" from white crackers instead of graham crackers. It gives it a cleaner, more springtime type of look without having to ice the whole house. I have tried it and it works very nicely. You do, however, need to be a little more careful with these type of crackers as they are a bit more fragile.

Windows

These are fun to create. Go to your local cake-decorating store and see what they have to offer in the way of hard flowers and candies made from icing. We were lucky enough to find carrots, flowers, bunnies, eggs and a tiny plastic wagon. We used two types of windows on our house, and both were very easy to do.

The one above the door is a round candy disc that you melt when you make candy. We placed that above the door, put a candy flower in the center of it and added two carrots that served as very nice looking shutters. Add a few tiny dots of icing and the look is complete.

The side windows are piped on with our decorator's tube so that we are able to add curtains and window dividers. We fashioned a window box using brown sugar wafer cookies and made shutters using pink sugar wafer cookies. We added candy flowers to the box and a few pastel M&M's above the window with icing dots to finish it off.

Porch Lights

We didn't want the Easter Bunny to trip on his way in, so we added two yellow gumdrop lights with icing dots to make them look just a little more fancy.

Flower Trellis

What spring cottage would be complete without a pretty flower trellis? Tint some icing pale green and pipe out lines of icing onto your house. You may want to do this in the back also. Add flowers made from icing, and you will be surprised how much color and life this adds to your house.

Trim Work

We lined all sides and seams of our house with tiny icing flowers. This really helps to brighten things up and make the house come alive.

Pathway

Our pathway is lined with beautiful flowers beckoning visitors to come in as our bunny looks out.

Roof

Instead of filling the roof with icing as we had always done before, we decided to put a decorator's tip on one of our icing tubes and pipe out a scalloped design on the roof. At each peak of the scallop, we added a tiny flower and topped the roof peak off with a beautiful row of spring posies.

Yard

We tinted some icing pale blue and added a tiny pond with duck crackers that we found in the grocery store. We added a little flower bed next to that, a small Easter basket and a small red wagon with a happy little gummy bear and foil-covered bunny.

BIRTHDAY BUNGALOW

What an unusual gift to give a child for their birthday! You can put a small present inside the house as you are building it or add a few extra special pieces of candy. The house is built the same way as the basic Holiday Wish House.

Windows

I wanted to use all of the candy that my daughter liked for her Birthday Bungalow. The windows were just piped on with a decorator's tube. Curtains were added and window boxes were fashioned from fudge bars. Tiny flowers were added to the boxes, and dots of icing and M&M's were added around the windows.

We found some chocolate hearts and added them to the corners of the house. Shutters were made from bits of graham crackers with icing piped on them to make them look more realistic.

Corner Decorations

She loves Pez®, so we added them to the corners of the house. They made it look as if the house were trimmed with corner stones.

Door

The front door is another graham cracker with a fruit slice placed above it to add some color. Another chocolate heart and some icing dots were also placed on the door, with an M&M as a doorknob.

Yard

We made the doormat from a wafer cookie and piped our daughter's name on it with icing.

The path is a simple one made from M&M's.

There is a tiny pond with a few red fish floating to the top to say "Happy Birthday."

We made some horses cut out of cookies and placed them in the pasture.

There are a few peppermint shrubs and a small wishing well made from M&M's.

The cookie roof is held up with pretzel sticks, and the tiny gumdrop bucket is held by some string licorice.

She not only has an unusual "Birthday Bungalow" but a special surprise inside and a wishing well where many wonderful wishes can come true.

CHAPTER 15

Gifts
and
Ideas

 # Gifts and Ideas

Now that you are an expert on making Holiday Wish Houses, here are a few ideas on other ways to use them. I know that there isn't a child around that wouldn't love to have a house like this for the holidays. But you would be surprised at the number of times that I have heard from adults, "I have always wanted one of those for the holidays," but, "They always seem too hard to make ," or "My mother would never have been able to do that!" Well, now you know how easy it is to do! I bet you can probably think of a number of adults who would love to have a Holiday Wish House of their very own.

GRANDMA AND GRAMPS

How about Grandma and Gramps? Sometimes it is so difficult to find just the right gift for them. Wouldn't it be nice to give them a Wish House to decorate their holiday table? It is especially nice if the children decorate one just for Grandma and Gramps. It makes it even more special. If they are on a special diet and you are concerned that they will do a little too much nibbling, use dietetic candies, sugar-free candies or just cookies and crackers. No matter what you use, I'm sure that they will love it.

DONATIONS

One project that I like to do every year involves two special groups—senior citizens and hospitalized children. I donate one Holiday Wish House for every nurses' station at the hospital. Instead of decorating every house by myself, I take a pre-assembled, undecorated house on a foil-covered base, bags of different candies and bags of icing to the seniors in the retirement home. The people at the retirement home do all of the decorating. It is wonderful to see their eyes light up at the idea of making the holidays a little more special for the children at the hospital. I have to admit that it is a difficult task for some of them to complete because of different health problems. But I think that by the time they finish their houses, they feel healthier and happier than they did before. I also take along a portable cassette player and play holiday music to help make the occasion a little more festive. At the end of the decorating, each person fills out a special Holiday Wish House card. The card says that the house was "Elf-made Especially For..." This adds an extra special magic to the whole event. They all smile as they put their names on the cards, knowing that they are the special elf that will bring holiday magic into a sick child's life.

Included in this book is a copy of the Elf-made Card. I hope it brings a smile to someone special.

FUND-RAISING

These houses may also be used as a fund-raiser for your local womens' or church group. You can do it a number of ways. One way is, of course, to sell the house fully decorated with an Official Holiday Wish House Certificate. You can ask a higher price for them selling them this way. Another way is to sell a pre-assembled, but undecorated, house on a foil-covered base. Along with it, give the customer a Magic Icing recipe, Official Certificate and a small bag of candy just to get them started. This is also nice because it will give the family a chance to decorate the house together.

Also, when the house is sold in kit form, it can be sold at a cheaper price, making it more attractive to more people. You may also want to try offering a workshop. Get together with a group of friends first and practice making the houses until you feel confident that you can make the presentation to your guests in a simple and pleasing manner. You may want to advertise in a local newspaper or church or school bulletin. Offer some light refreshments such as coffee and cookies or punch and dessert.

Fill the air with pleasant holiday sounds and add a few decorations to the room. To save time, you may want to present each person with a pre-assembled house. You can demonstrate the procedure so that they understand the basic idea. Have the icing ready in disposable bags. By having the icing ready, you know that it is the right consistency. Ask that they bring their own candies as they may have their favorites. There you go, a room full of happy people, good food and lovely music.

What more could you ask for?

SCOUT TROOPS AND OTHER GROUPS

How many times around the holidays have you looked for something different for your Scout troop to do and not been able to come up with an original idea? Why not try this? I have done this with Girl Scouts, Brownies, Cub Scouts, Indian Princesses, and Boy Scouts. The girls all enjoyed it very much; and to my surprise, the boys LOVED it! This is not a usual activity for most boys to get to do. Many of the Scout leaders said that it was the quietest meeting they had ever had! Hard to believe, but it's true.

Because of time limitations, I would go prepared when I would do a group like the Scouts. I would tell the leaders that I would bring everything except the candy. That meant an undecorated pre-assembled house on a foil-covered base, a bag of icing for each child , a few houses just in case, my cassette player with holiday music, scissors and a little Christmas tree for each child.

Remind the children to be gentle with their houses. Tell them the procedure for decorating front, sides, back, roof and, lastly, the yard. Also point out that the weakest parts of the house are the roof seams and the end tips.

Since there are a lot of colds this time of year, it is best to give each child a bowl of assorted candies. They may then swap with each other if they wish.

They are all so proud of themselves when they go home, and the parents seem very pleased that they now have an added holiday decoration.

Certificate

of

Holiday Wishes

Elfmade Especially for

**Close Your Eyes
Make a Wish
And It May Just Come True**

CHAPTER 16

Holiday Traditions

 # Holiday Traditions

Once again, I am back to the very reason for starting this whole idea in the first place–a special holiday tradition, something that you can do year after year; something that can grow with friends and family; something that your children and loved ones will remember for years to come.

Send out party invitations to some of your childrens' friends. I have included six in this book. Your children can color them, add stickers or create their own.

Once the invitations are out, pre-assemble your houses and gather your candies. Make your icing and put it in the bags the day of the party. Make sure to tape the ends shut tight so that when the children begin to squeeze the icing out, it doesn't come out the wrong end.

You may want to serve hot chocolate and have some soft holiday music playing in the background. Then stand back and watch the children create their own wonderful dream-come-true.

You may also want to invite some of the parents and friends to help you decorate your tree while the children are busy.

Every year you will find more wonderful things to add to make your party even more special. However you decide to use this idea, I hope that you warm the hearts and light up the eyes of the people and children that you love.

To Make a
Holiday Wish House

WHO:_____

WHERE:_____

DATE: _____

TIME:_____

R.S.V.P.:_____

You Are
Invited

To Make a
Holiday Wish House

WHO:_____

WHERE:_____

DATE: _____

TIME:_____

R.S.V.P.: _____

You Are
Invited

To Make a
Holiday Wish House

WHO:_____

WHERE:_____

DATE: _____

TIME:_____

R.S.V.P.:_____

You Are
Invited

To Make a
Holiday Wish House

WHO:_____

WHERE:_____

DATE: _____

TIME:_____

R.S.V.P.: _____

You Are
Invited

To Make a
Holiday Wish House

WHO:_____

WHERE:_____

DATE: _____

TIME:_____

R.S.V.P.: _____

You Are
Invited

To Make a Holiday Wish House

WHO: _____

WHERE: _____

DATE: _____

TIME: _____

R.S.V.P.: _____

You Are
Invited

To Make a
Holiday Wish House

WHO:_____

WHERE:_____

DATE: _____

TIME: _____

R.S.V.P.:_____

You Are Invited

To Make a
Holiday Wish House

WHO:_____

WHERE:_____

DATE: _____

TIME:_____

R.S.V.P.: _____

You Are
Invited